WORLD WAR II
Dispatches to Madison

WORLD WAR II

Dispatches to Madison

LETTERS HOME FROM
AN ARMY AIR CORPS SOLDIER

DANNELLE GAY

THE
History
PRESS

Published by The History Press
Charleston, SC
www.historypress.com

All images from the author's family collection.

First published 2024

Manufactured in the United States

ISBN 9781467157186

Library of Congress Control Number: 2024931561

Notice: The information in this book is true and complete to the best of our knowledge. It is offered without guarantee on the part of the author or The History Press. The author and The History Press disclaim all liability in connection with the use of this book.

To anyone who has ever put on a uniform for Uncle Sam—we thank you.
We know this is simply one story of many who have served,
but all are worthy. That is why I am donating all profits from this book
to the Wounded Warrior Project.

CONTENTS

HOW HAS YOUR JOURNEY GONE SO FAR?

We take for granted what our journey in life should contain. We want it filled with pictures of our children and grandchildren, mixed in with some sights and sounds of our furry little friends (kitties and pups), sprinkled with some panoramic views from the world realm or sharing a comfy backyard fire on a crisp October evening with some of our closest friends.

The type of journey you are about to digest here is so much more than that! It encompasses more than just "memories" of a trip we may have had with kith and kin. It dives deep into our souls. It is a shared experience between families and friends, the type of journey that comes once a generation… when war comes to call.

Sometimes, I delve into my own genealogy to help frame my personal expedition in life. For instance, how did it feel for my great-great-granduncle, Dennis Riley (maternal side), as he walked into Camp Randall and enlisted as a soldier in Company Bravo, Seventh Wisconsin Volunteer Infantry during the Civil War? He knew the Union needed him to fight for the freedom of everyone. Little did anyone anticipate that he would be wounded in the Siege of Petersburg and live out his final days in (Medina) Marshall, Wisconsin, only to die at forty-nine years of age.

This type of journey would repeat itself a generation later on my paternal side, where great-uncles Emil and Joe Parr, as well as Lawrence and Norbert Motl, all put on uniforms to fight in World War II. Those types of journeys took loved ones away and painted a different reality for friends, family and community. They carry on in the eyes of their children and replicate every time there is war.

The author, Dannelle Gay, is a local icon in Wisconsin. She is a TV host, published author, public speaker and world traveler. Her critiques of local and international destinations are beyond reproach. Her journeys are well documented.

This composition of work sheds light on what every generation has had to live with in perpetuity, from General Burgoyne to Petraeus. This is a very personal journey that her father-in-law had with World War II as the backdrop. The general anxiety of that relationship can be repeated countlessly throughout our collective history. We can look at her father-in-law through the lens of a young man; an anxious warrior (soldier); a wanderer; a melancholy soul; a joyful perpetrator of the future; a man who holds with beliefs of duty, honor and country; a man filled with uncertainty about what the future holds; and most importantly, a man who loves his family.

What makes it memorable and meaningful is that we can celebrate the strengths and frailties of our neighbors, friends and family members. We can identify parallels with what we are experiencing.

In essence, our journey is enriched because we know and acknowledge their journeys. That makes this collection all the more potent, exceptional, authentic. It adds value to all of us.

Enjoy!
Thomas J. Parr

•————•

Thomas J. Parr is currently the Southwest Wisconsin regional director for the Wisconsin Veterans Chamber of Commerce. He works to advance business opportunities for veterans and vet-friendly businesses. He currently resides in Madison, Wisconsin, with his lovely wife, Susan, and their two sons, Caden and Gavin. He has known Dannelle for a brief moment in time but feels as if he has "known" her his entire life.

ACKNOWLEDGEMENTS

I would like to express my deepest gratitude to the individuals who made this book possible:

Teenagers Noel and Mika, who painstakingly typed up six journals full of old World War II letters and V-Mails. They brought to life the personal story of this young man who served and the friends he would make along the way. On Sunday, February 21, 1943, you will meet Jerry Gredler from Milwaukee, who became a lifelong pal. On June 11, 1944, you will learn of Tom Jones, who would become Bob's best man when he got married after the war. These and so many more soldiers grace these pages.

Thanks to Kyle Wege of Crimson Sun Studios, who breathed new life into the old and fading photographs, allowing us to see the faces of those who sacrificed so much of their early adult lives.

Then there is my new friend Thomas Parr, who wrote the foreword and works for the Wisconsin Veterans Chamber of Commerce. He brought his expertise and passion for history to the project, as well as helped me curate a list of organizations to help fellow veterans.

I can't forget The History Press and how they took a chance on this book, and for that, I am forever grateful.

Finally, I would like to thank Bob's mother, who meticulously archived all the information that we share in the following pages. Her dedication and hard work made this book possible and ensured that the stories of those who served will never be forgotten. You will learn how she and Bob's dad would often ask if Bob's fellow soldiers needed anything—if they could send extra care packages, etc. They would make multiple sets of pictures from the film Bob sent home so they could mail back copies of the photos for each soldier to have their own. They even got addresses of other parents to connect with—all while being on the local ration board, serving with the USO, helping the Red Cross, having a large victory garden, keeping the family businesses going, pulling off a wedding for their daughter and so much more.

As Bob would say: "They sure were swell folks."

AUTHOR'S NOTE

Dear reader,

In the heart of Madison, Wisconsin, the Gay family emerged as true pillars of the community, leaving an indelible mark that stretched far beyond bricks and mortar. Their legacy was etched into the cityscape, defining an era of progress and philanthropy.

The crowning jewel of their accomplishments was the construction of the first Madison skyscraper, the Gay Building, which today stands as the renowned Churchill Building at 16 North Carroll Street. This nine-story architectural marvel symbolized their unwavering commitment to modernity and progress. But their contributions extended well beyond the city's skyline.

Throughout Madison's neighborhoods, the Gay family's influence was felt on a deeply personal level. They weren't just builders of structures; they were builders of communities. Scores of commercial buildings, homes and apartment buildings, each bearing the mark of their dedication to quality and design, sprang up in downtown Madison, along Monroe Street and in the cherished Dudgeon neighborhood.

Yet their legacy extended even further. The Gay family's philanthropic spirit was evident in their generous donations of land to Madison for significant community projects. The Dudgeon School, an institution that has educated generations, stands on land gifted by the Gays. A part of what is now the picturesque Tenney Park, a haven for Madison residents, also carries their legacy. And in a gesture of enduring environmental stewardship, their partnership with the Lake Forest Land Company resulted in a contribution to the esteemed UW Arboretum, enriching Madison's natural beauty for generations to come.

But even as they built, the Gays recognized the importance of accessibility. To ensure that residents of their new developments could easily reach the heart of the city for work and leisure, they founded the Madison Bus Trust, a visionary initiative that served as a lifeline connecting the community to their dreams and aspirations.

The Gay brothers, led by the patriarch Leonard Gay Sr., were five dynamic individuals who each played a unique role in shaping Madison's destiny. Leonard Jr., David, John, Sydney and Randall collectively forged a family legacy that became synonymous with progress and community-building.

However, like many families of their time, they were not untouched by the trials of their era. The tumultuous years of World War I took a toll on their lives, as it did for countless families across the nation. Not all the brothers returned home the same, and their experiences during the war left lasting scars.

The subsequent Great Depression, coupled with the challenges of a failed partnership with the Lake Forest Land Company, marked the end of an era for the family's grand ambitions. Though they held on to their existing holdings, the business never quite transitioned to the next generation.

As the clouds of World War II gathered on the horizon, casting a shadow over the world, the fate of the Gay family's fortunes hung in the balance. Whether World War II played a role in the family's business trajectory remains a mystery, one of many unanswered questions in the tapestry of their history.

Yet their legacy endures, not only in the structures that grace Madison's streets but also in the spirit of community and innovation that continues to define this vibrant city. The Gay family's story is a testament to the enduring values of vision, philanthropy and resilience that have left an indelible mark on Madison, a mark that will be forever etched in its history.

This book delves into the extraordinary journey of Leonard Gay Jr.'s family, with a particular focus on his only son, Robert. Through the pages of Robert's heartfelt letters sent home during his time in the Army Air Corps in World War II, we uncover a young man's transformation from a local Madison boy to a courageous soldier serving on European soil.

Robert's letters speak not only of duty and patriotism but also of love. Like countless GIs of his time, he left behind a girlfriend, only to lose her during the trials of war. Yet through his furloughs and travels, he discovered new friendships and connections, until finally, he returned home to marry a childhood friend who became his sweetheart.

In the midst of it all, Robert's humility shone bright. Years later, he hesitated to accept a spot on the Badger Honor Flight—the local honor flight that takes veterans for a trip to Washington, D.C., to see the monuments that stand in their honor and provides a celebratory welcome home that many never saw—believing that others were more deserving. Eventually, he relented and embarked on a journey that would become one of the highlights of his life.

Though Robert is no longer with us, his legacy lives on through these poignant letters. He was a kind, generous soul who loved his family, friends and country. What you are about to read is a tribute to him and to all the brave men and women who have served our nation.

Moreover, this book is not just a story; it's also a mission. All my profits from this endeavor will be donated to the Wounded Warrior Project, in honor of Robert's belief that "other fellas deserved it more." He may not be here to say it, but we believe he'd find this endeavor "swell."

So the next time you stroll through the Dane County Farmer's Market, gaze upon the Churchill Building or take a leisurely walk in the UW Arboretum, we hope you'll remember Bob and his unwavering dedication. These were the places he loved and fought for, and his story is a testament to the enduring spirit of Madison and its people.

Enjoy this journey through history, love and honor as we share the extraordinary story of Robert Gay and his remarkable family.

Please keep in mind that we typed up his letters exactly as they were written. English wasn't his strongest subject in high school. Read past the missing comma or occasionally misspelled word—you won't be sorry.

Dannelle Gay
Bob's daughter-in-law

Bob (*left*) in his World War II uniform and his dad, Len, in his World War I uniform, photographed on Bob's first furlough.

INTRODUCTION

Bob stood nervously outside his dad's office door, the weight of his decision heavy on his shoulders. He took a deep breath and knocked gently. The door opened a crack, revealing his father, Leonard, hunched over his desk, engrossed in paperwork.

"Dad, do you have a minute?"

Without looking up, Leonard put down his pen and smiled warmly at his son. "Hey there, Bob. Of course I've got a minute for my favorite son. What's on your mind?"

Bob stepped into the room, closing the door behind him. He shifted from foot to foot, struggling to find the right words.

"Dad, I've been thinking. My friends are enlisting in the army, and I want to do my part too. I want to join up."

Leonard's expression shifted, and he walked over to the window, gazing out at the world beyond. He remained silent for a few minutes, lost in thought. Was he thinking about his own service in World War I? Was he thinking of his only son facing something similar? No one will ever know.

Finally, he turned back to Bob, a mixture of pride and concern in his eyes.

He said softly, "You know, Bob, you're growing up so fast. This world is changing, and it's a scary time. But before you make any decisions, can you do me a favor?"

Bob nodded, his heart pounding in his chest. "Sure, Dad, anything."

"Tell your mom your favorite meals, although I'm sure she's more than aware. Date a pretty girl or two, and take some walks with Yippee in the woods. Enjoy just being a teenager for the moment. Before you head off into the unknown, there's a lot of life to live. I guarantee you, Uncle Sam will send an invitation soon enough."

Bob's eyes welled up with emotion as he absorbed his father's words.

"Okay, Dad. I promise."

Six weeks later, the fateful letter arrived. Bob opened it with trembling hands and read the words that would change his life forever. Uncle Sam had indeed extended his "invitation." As he held the letter in his hands, he thought back to that heartfelt conversation with his dad and knew that he was about to embark on a journey that would test his courage, strength and the love of his family.

Prepare in Duplicate

App. not Req.

DEC 30 1942
(Date of mailing)

ORDER TO REPORT FOR INDUCTION

The President of the United States,

To   Robert   Lee   Gay
      (First name)   (Middle name)   (Last name)

Order No.   12596

GREETING:

Having submitted yourself to a local board composed of your neighbors for the purpose of determining your availability for training and service in the armed forces of the United States, you are hereby

notified that you have now been selected for training and service in the _____ Army _____
(Army, Navy, Marine Corps)

You will, therefore, report to the local board named above at Rm 305, Washington Bldg.,
119 E. Washington Avenue, Madison, Wis.
(Place of reporting)

at   6:30   A. m., on the 9th (Saturday) day of January _____, 19 43.
(Hour of reporting)

This local board will furnish transportation to an induction station of the service for which you have been selected.
You will there be examined, and, if accepted for training and service, you will then be inducted into the stated branch of the service.

Persons reporting to the induction station in some instances may be rejected for physical or other reasons. It is well to keep this in mind in arranging your affairs, to prevent any undue hardship if you are rejected at the induction station. If you are employed, you should advise your employer of this notice and of the possibility that you may not be accepted at the induction station. Your employer can then be prepared to replace you if you are accepted, or to continue your employment if you are rejected.

Willful failure to report promptly to this local board at the hour and on the day named in this notice is a violation of the Selective Training and Service Act of 1940, as amended, and subjects the violator to fine and imprisonment.

If you are so far removed from your own local board that reporting in compliance with this order will be a serious hardship and you desire to report to a local board in the area of which you are now located, go immediately to that local board and make written request for transfer of your delivery for induction, taking ____ ___ with you.

D. S. S. Form 150
(Revised 7-13-42)

U. S. GOVERNMENT PRINTING OFFICE : 1942   16—16271-4

SELECTIVE SERVICE
STATE HEADQUARTERS
122 West Washington Avenue
Madison, Wisconsin

MEMORANDUM TO SELECTEES

You have just received your notice to report for induction into the Armed Forces of the United States. Within a few days you will report at your Local Board office to be sent to the U. S. Army Induction Station.

It is not necessary that you take any personal equipment with you to the Induction Station unless you are required to spend the night in a hotel prior to induction or elect to be sent direct to the Reception Center after induction.

The following is a suggested list of personal items you should take with you if you elect to go to the Reception Center immediately after induction or when recalled to service as a Reservist, (termination of furlough).

In addition to clothing worn by selectee -

    Shaving kit
    1 bar soap
    Tooth brush with paste or powder
    Bath towels
    2 suits underwear
    Sox
    Handkerchiefs

You should provide yourself with a small container or handbag in which to carry the above articles. Trunk or suitcase will not be taken. Barrack Bag will be issued at the Reception Center.

Within 24 hours after arrival at the Reception Center, you will be issued clothing and other personal equipment.

Intoxicating liquor of any kind is forbidden on buses or trains and if found in your possession enroute may cause your arrest. Intoxication will not be tolerated.

Be courteous and gentlemanly in your conduct at all times. This is one of the first qualities of the American Soldier.

For the Governor:

John F. Mullen

JOHN F. MULLEN
Colonel, Infantry
State Director

JFM:MZ

Top: Bob's invitation from Uncle Sam.

Bottom: Draft letter insert on FAQs.

CHAPTER 1

FORT SHERIDAN, ILLINOIS

January 19, 1943

Dear Dad, Mom, and Kath:

How are you? Fine, I hope.

I like the army fine so far. We get darn good food, considering it is not "home cooking." We get fresh fruit every meal, meat, potatoes, milk, coffee, sugar, peanut butter, vegetables, jelly, bread, all kinds of seasoning, and even cocoa once. We don't get this all at once, but the meals are very well planned. The things are seasoned a little too much to suit me, but we are so hungry by mealtime that we would eat anything.

We sure have a lot of equipment and we will get more when we get wherever we are sent.

We finished our processing today. I am not sure yet, but I think I am going to be put into the Air Corps Ground Forces. I repeat, I am not at all sure yet.

We arrived here around noon, Saturday, and were assigned barracks. This was after a bumpy ride about $\frac{1}{2}$ or $\frac{3}{4}$ of a mile packed in a truck. We then got our bunks assigned to us. We had lights out about 9:15. Got us up at 7 o'clock the next morning. It was Sunday and that is why we stayed until 7:00.

On Sunday, we got our clothes, etc. For processing we went first to hear the articles of war, then, on Monday, to our tests, on which I didn't do so bad. I got a high enough grade to be eligible

R E S T R I C T E D

E X T R A C T

SO 8-5 Hq. Milwaukee District, U.S.Army Recruiting & Induction Service
234 North Broadway, Milwaukee, isconsin, dd 9 January, 1943.

6. Each of the following named EM, inducted into the US, this date,
is released fr AD, and is trfd to the ERC and P to Madison, Wisconsin.

NAME	ASN	NAME	ASN
WOLF, JOSEPH	36296379	SCHALLER, JAMES A.	36296380
RAND, MYRTON C.	36296381	WAGNER, VERNON P.	36296382
DORR, GLENN A.	36296383	BONNER, DONALD J.	36296384
RYAN, WALLACE J.	36296385	FOLLETT, ALLAN W.	36296386
ROMINE, JAMES H.	36296387	MILLER, CHESTER F.	36296388
KRAUSE, WILLIAM L.	36296389	BREITENBACH, MARCUS W.	36296390
STENSON, GAROLD G.	36296391	CARBERRY, THOMAS H.	36296392
CARPENTER, PAUL E.	36296393	DENIS, JACK A.	36296394
RYAN, FRANCIS B.	36296395	SCHUSTER, AARON	36296396
CLEMENS, STANLEY J.	36296397	SANDERSON, WILLIAM D.	36296398
FAHEY, JAMES V.	36296399	MANTHE, FRED W.	36296400
GEORGESON, GEORGE R.R.	36296401	BONINO, JOE S.	36296402
CARUSO, JOHN J.	36296403	EGGERS, THOMAS A.	36296404
GROVER, HALE W.	36296405	WILHELM, ROBERT F.	36296406
GAY, ROBERT L.	36296407	ROSS, ROMAN W.	36296408
STASSI, CHARLES S.	36296409	AUDINI, ROY E.	36296410
SCOTT, CHARLES J.	36296411	JACKSON, JR. ARNOLD S.	36296412
CALIVA, GEORGE	36296413	LARSEN, FRANK J.	36296414
USHER, GLENN D.	36296415	SPETH, KARL F.	36296416
GLAGOW, WILLIAM F.	36296417LS	KELLER, WILLIAM R.	36296418LS
HAMACHEK, RUSSELL H.	36296419LS	KELLY, LEWIS B.	36296420LS

Effective January 16, 1943, each of the above named EM of the ERC is
called to AD and WP from Madison, Wisconsin, to Fort Sheridan, Illinois,
rpt upon arrival thereat, to the CO, RRC, for duty.
QMC NT. TDN FD 31 P 431-02 A 0425-23.

By Order of Lt. Col. GOFFARD

JESS W. BLACK
Captain, Infantry
Asst. Rctg. & Ind.Officer

R E S T R I C T E D

Bob's orders to Fort Sheridan, Illinois.

for officers training, however there are many more things to be considered before that could happen. That was my I.Q. test.

Today we got our insurance and bond payments taken care of and also our shots. If you find this hard to read, it is partly because my arm is awfully stiff from a typhoid shot and also because I am writing on a bed. Enclosed you will find my insurance receipts and bond receipts. I took out a $10,000 policy and will get one $25.00 bond a month. This bond will take place of the money I was going to send home. My insurance costs me $6.50 per month and the bond costs $18.75. This still leaves me enough money for my needs. I made Kath co-owner of the bonds. They will be mailed to her. I want Pop to put them in the bank with my others. I doubt if any will come before the first part of March.

I hope none of you are working too hard. I'll write more whenever I get time. Plenty of the boys are feeling sick as a result of the shots. We had awful chills, not all of us but quite a few, including myself. I'm feeling fine now though so don't worry.

Love, Bob

CHAPTER 2

ST. PETERSBURG, FLORIDA

January 23, 1943

Dear folks:

Guess where I am? I'm in St. Petersburg, Florida, only three blocks from Uncle John and Aunt Maude! I called them on the phone about 25 minutes ago. Were they ever surprised.

We are in the U.S. Army Air Corps. We will be classified again and then put in certain branches of the Air Corps. We arrived here at 2 a.m. today. Stood around and then had to march to a large building for a physical check-up. Then we were assigned to hotels, of which the army controls most. I am now at a large 7 or 8 story modern hotel. It used to be the Soreno Hotel, but is now the 603rd Technical School Squadron. It is very modern and is seven stories high. It overlooks Tampa Bay.

Is the weather ever wonderful, warm, refreshing and sunny. We left Fort Sheridan Wednesday evening at 9 o'clock p.m. Rode to Chicago, changed trains, rode on down through Kentucky, Tennessee, Georgia and then Florida. Sat up in the seats all the way. Slept sitting in seats, did not have clothes off all the way. I just had a shower, and boy! Do I ever feel better.

Food not bad, but sure miss Mom's cooking! I'm going to see John and Maude as soon as possible, but when I can I hope we can go and get a big steak. This sure is a nice place, flowers out, green grass, leaves, etc. Keep us awful busy. Hope I get more time to write tomorrow. I sure miss good Wisconsin milk and butter. Little butter here and milk once a day. Drank coffee on the train for two days. Yuck. Feel pretty fair, considering my cold and lack of sleep. Will even get another G.I. hair cut here. You should see me, wow! I'll write more tomorrow.

Love Bob

·———·

January 24, 1943

Dear Dad, Mom and Kath:

I'm in the Army Air Forces for sure. I will be here for at least 4 weeks and maybe more. We receive our basic training here. We have kept very busy since we arrived here, listening to lectures, etc. Tomorrow we take exams, and if we pass the Army Air Corps will send us to a technical training school. What it will be, radio, mechanical, or whatever, the tests will determine. There are quite a number of these schools. I sure hope I can make one O.K.

Here is my address:

Pvt. Robert L. Gay, 36296407
604 T.S.S. A.A.F. Flight 288
St. Petersburg, Florida

PLEASE WRITE.

Pepper, Usher, and Speth were still at Fort Sheridan when I left there. Only a couple or three fellows here that I knew fairly well.

I sure do miss your cooking, Mom, but what we get isn't so bad. I've learned to eat almost anything even drink some coffee, if there isn't milk or water around. I can call Aunt Maude and Uncle John about every night, but will not be able to get a pass to see them until the coming weekend because we are in quarantine for five or six days.

I wrote cards to Gay Bros., Grandma Gay, Grandma Lee, the Sasmans and a letter to Barbara today. Wouldn't it be funny if I made a radio school and got sent to Truax Field? You can never tell. However, the chances are so small so far as being sent so close to home is concerned. How's your back, Mom? Take care of it won't you?

Write soon, good night,

Love, Bob

.————.

January 27, 1943

Dear folks:

Well another day, another sore arm. We get another typhoid shot today, and also a blood type test. My blood is type A. We always get a sore arm from these typhoid shots. We are really starting to get it now. Drill, lectures and calisthenics all day.

Tomorrow, I will know whether or not I will eventually be sent to an Air Force Technical School. Also what kind of training I will get—radio, airplane mechanic, armorer, gunner, radio mech., and so on. If I get a choice I believe I will take radio.

The Air Corps has what is called an "emergency furlough." We have been instructed to write home about it. In case anything serious happens such as an accident, death, serious sickness, etc. in the family or near friends, you should call the Red Cross in Madison and tell them you want me to come home. Give them my full name and address (if you know it at the time), just my name and serial number will do. Always give my serial number.

To get me home on that furlough, it must be an emergency.

Remember to call the Red Cross in Madison, not where I am. The Red Cross will take care of the rest. They say they will really get us home in a hurry. O.K. now that's done. We were told to let you know how to get us home just in case.

I believe I will get my first pass Thursday night. If I do I am going to eat with Uncle John and Aunt Maude. Today was a special day here. We had peanut butter to put on the bread. The food here is healthy but not nearly as good as at Fort Sheridan.

Did you receive those papers? I hope so. I am glad that I am buying one $25.00 bond per month. They deduct $18.75 a month for the bond and $6.50 per month for insurance. You see

Bob with the girl he was dating at the beginning of the war; this is either the Barbara (Bobbie) or Jackie he mentions in his letters.

I will have $25.25 deducted from my pay and will receive $24.75 each month. I can get along on this O.K. I sure hope so anyway. I believe I will need that money more after the war than I do now.

Naturally I miss you all, but this is how it has to be. Say Mom, I can really eat almost anything now. We get so hungry that we eat everything but the tray. Darn few cars running around here.

All of us sent here are supposed to be the cream of the crop, so far as intelligence shown in the army tests is concerned.

Good night,

Love, Bob

·————·

January 31, 1943

Dear Pop, Mom and Kath:

I had dinner and supper with Aunt Maude and Uncle John, today. Had swell meals. I feel swell and am having fun. We work plenty hard now, but even so I like it. Aunt Maude took some snapshots of me today.

Beautiful town and wonderful weather. I've got a nice sunburn already. In three weeks I should be tall, tan and plenty strong. The obstacle course is really something! This is what we have to do:

(1) Jump fence touching hands only, (2) Must climb smooth 10 ft. wall and jump down, (3) Must run up steep ramp and jump down, (4) Must jump ditch, (5) Must crawl through small enclosed places on hands and feet, (6) Must swing hand to hand over a deep pit on rods, (7) Must cross pit by putting legs and hands around rope and push across another smooth wall. All of this takes $\frac{1}{4}$ mile, and is run on soft sand, which is the worst obstacle because of the work it makes of running. I made it O.K. the first time, but was plenty tired. I'll get it O.K., don't worry about that. I got a swell letter from Barbara today, and it sure made me awful happy. I think she is wonderful. It is my first letter from home. I hope to hear from you tomorrow. Aunt Maude let me read your last letter to her. Please take good care of your cold, Mom, and Mom, please don't worry about me as they take good care of us here. I got a room last night. I have been sleeping in the hall, because there were so many boys here. I am really in a suite of

two rooms, in which are 11 boys, five in my room and six in the other. One bath between us.

Happy Birthday, Mom. I know I'm late, but I was so busy I guess I forgot. I even have it written down in my book. I'm sorry I forgot.

Love, Bob

.———.

February 3, 1943

Dear Kath:

Thanks a lot for the swell letter. I got it today about 5:20 p.m. I will eventually get an Air Corps insignia which is a round button with a propeller and wings on it. It will be on the lapel of my suit coat. I will also have an Air Corps emblem on my shoulder like the soldiers have in Madison. We cannot wear these until we are shipped to school.

I hope you made all of your exams. O.K.—I know you did.

It really sounds as if you are going places. I hope you had fun on your date.

I really got a swell letter from Mom, yesterday, the long typed one. It sure makes me feel good to hear from home.

Enclosed, you will find a little Air Corps pin which I bought for you. I hope it will not be bent or broken when it arrives. Also hope you like it.

Have Mom and Pop read the whole letter, won't you?

Hello Mom and Pop, our whole flight had its passes pulled today. We can't go out for two days, because our rooms did not pass inspection this a.m. It is O.K. though, because I can get some writing done. Today we had over two hours of exercises, hours and hours of drill, ran the obstacle course, and got another shot in the arm. *I feel good*. Still have slight cold though.

Temperature here is over 80 degrees. Plenty warm.

Love, Bob

.———.

February 4, 1943

Dear Kath:

I received that nifty letter that you wrote at "Rainbow." Thanks a lot. It was very interesting to say the least! Please say "Hello" to Iola, Marsh, Jones etc., and thank them for their notes. It was certainly nice of them.

I'm glad you had fun on that date. Are you sure it's the boy and not the car? I wonder. Maybe it's a combination of both that you like.

Please let Mom and Pop read this too.

Dear Dad, Mom and Kath and Yippee too:

How is everyone? Hope Mom's cold is better. Is it Mom?

The army got very generous today, for breakfast we had some "ole" [the family's name for oleo] to put on the toast. That is the nearest thing to butter, since we reached here. Tonight we even had some jelly, and boy, did it ever taste good.

We can't go out again tonight because the 6th floor wasn't clean. I hope we can get passes tomorrow night, so I can see Uncle John and Aunt Maude. We got kicked out of the writing room, tonight, and thus I am sitting on the floor in the hall under the little exit light so I can see to write. You see, it is after lights out and these are the only lights that stay on. We can stay up until eleven, but lights are out at nine, except in the recreation room downstairs.

We had a really tough day today. The work is tougher every day. We had calisthenics, drill, obstacle course, drill some more and then more calisthenics. Then we paraded at retreat. Kept on our feet from 6:30 a.m. to 12:00, and from 12:45 to 5:30 p.m. Everyone is stiff and we all have tired feet, however I feel pretty good. I sure do eat. Even when the food is bad I eat most of it, because I am so hungry. The temperature today was around 90. I like it warm. I sure have a nice sunburn, not very sore tho. Will write tomorrow.

Love, Bob

•———————•

February 13, 1943

Dear folks:

I saw Grandma Gay, last night, and she looks fine after her trip. Aunt Maude, Grandma, Uncle John and I had a nice visit. I stayed there until about 10:00 p.m. at which time I could hardly keep my eyes open as we had had a tough day. Grandma gave me your special delivery letter, Mom. It was swell. It sounds as though you were keeping awfully busy, Mom. I hope you are having fun. Don't worry about a letter a day, because I know that you are busy and when I get a nice long one like the one you wrote Sunday, it makes up for a number of days.

I feel swell and am getting along fine. Uncle John and Aunt Maude are doing so much for me. She gave me two wash rags, a case for my glasses and they buy me swell meals on Sunday, when I can be with them.

Lots of the fellows that came here with me are being shipped already. I may be shipped any day, now. We never know.

I'll bet your new clothes look neat, Pop. Looks as though you will have to be careful of everything, doesn't it? Well, don't worry about me, because my clothes are pretty new yet, and I suppose there are more for me to have if these wear out. My "Uncle" [Sam] has a few boys here to outfit so he's kept rather busy.

I'd sure like to see the new office, Pop. I'll bet it's a honey. I'm sure glad I had my teeth fixed before I got here. Thanks for paying the bill.

I got paid $13.50 on Friday. Still have plenty of money.

When we got back to the hotel last evening at 4:30 p.m. we had to go on K.P. [kitchen patrol, working under the kitchen staff] again. I worked until 6 o'clock this morning. I was up over 25 hours, and am plenty tired this a.m. I slept until 11:30 and then went to eat dinner with the John Gays and Grandma. I returned to the hotel around 2 o'clock and washed my fatigue suit, then Stanley (Red) Clemons and I went to a show, after which we both ate with the folks again. Aunt Maude and Uncle John just do too much for me. They won't let me pay for my dinners etc. I only get to eat with them on Sundays, though, because it is after six when we get our passes on weekdays.

Bob in St. Petersburg, Florida, on pass.

I've got a really nice gang in the room with me, now, but two are shipping tomorrow. I now have a mattress and pillow, it feels wonderful.

I got a package slip today, which means there is a package for me in the mail room, but I can't get it until morning. Maybe it's the cookies from Eunice. Grandma, John and Maude look fine and all seem happy. Say "Hello" to everyone for me. I'll write again soon.

Love, Bob

.————.

February 16, 1943

Hi Everyone:

Well another day and another dollar and sixty-six and two-thirds cents. No pay for overtime, but that doesn't mean that we don't get any. I worked on K.P. two night inside of five days. One day I was up 24 hours and then 25 hours the other day. I have also had guard duty from 10 to 12 p.m.

We didn't get out tonight, because the inspection officer found too many things wrong.

We sure are getting a real workout, but I like it. I eat plenty, but mainly because I'm so terribly hungry and not because the chow is so good.

I hope to get out to see Grandma and the John Gays tomorrow night. I have only seen Grandma twice, so far I believe. I have only four days left of my basic training, but if I'm not shipped to my school by then, I will start supplementary training. Almost half of the boys in my flight have been shipped. A few go every day.

The weather here has been pretty darn cool the last three days, but it is still awfully nice.

I sure would like to see your new office. I'll bet it is pretty nice. I hope you can read this, because I am so sleepy I can hardly keep my eyes open.

I'm hitting the hay.

Love, Bob

.————.

CHAPTER 3

TENT CITY, FLORIDA

Same Address Plus Tent City Area
February 21, 1943

Dear folks:

I have been moved out of St. Pete. I now live in "Tent City" on the edge of St. Pete. We were moved out here yesterday at 5:30 p.m. There are eight of us in each tent, and this is real army life. Nothing but tents for block upon block.

We eat outside all of the time and eat from our chow kits.

We sleep on army cots, no pillows, no blankets, no sheets. We have two comforters and that is all. We keep everything in the barracks bags. No place to hang anything up. Sleep in our clothes to help keep warm. It gets cool at night, but is plenty warm in the daytime. I believe it was 90 degrees F yesterday. This place is about six miles from my old home in St. Pete.

We are just back of the Jungle Hotel, which is a large place. This used to be a beautiful golf course, but is now just dirt and sand. It is as dirty a place as I have ever seen. When a truck or group of men go by it is so dusty you can hardly breathe.

I still feel swell, however, and am having fun. I am now all done with my basic training. We finished it yesterday. Friday we were on the range. We shot Thompson submachine guns and rifles. Then we went through the gas chamber. Used our gas masks. Learned to identify different kinds of gases by actually smelling weak samples of the gases, mustard gas etc. We will probably stay here until we get shipped. Less than ½ of our flight is left.

I will still get a pass to go to town now and then. We are just beyond the end of the street car line and can ride to town for 10¢ if we can get on the car.

You can see how dirty it is here by looking at the fingerprints on the paper. I hope you can read this letter O.K.

I got two letters from Mom, and one from Kath and Mom together, yesterday. Thanks a lot. I get some mail every day, isn't that swell? Say, Kath, that really was a neat valentine. O.K.! Kath, thanks very much for the letters you send me, however, don't neglect your studying because you better graduate so I can buy you a present. O.K.?

Yes, Mom, I did have my calisthenics on the beach in my undershirt, just like they did in Miami. I believe you asked me that. I'll get your letter out and answer your questions when I can. The weather is beautiful today.

I have a swell Buddy, now. His name is Gerald "Jerry" Gredler. Jerry is from South Milwaukee and is a swell kid. He came down with us, but I just got to know him a few days ago. He is about the same size as I am, nice fellow, He neither smokes or drinks so we get along fine. He is also supposed to go to radio school. We hope to go together.

That's all for now.

Love, Bob

•———•

February 26, 1943

Dear Dad, Mom and Kath:

How are you? That is one thing I don't hear much about. I feel swell and I'm not kidding. Right this minute I'm sitting behind my tent with my shirt off getting a swell tan.

We are doing very little these days. Just waiting to be shipped. A few boys go each day, so you never can tell when I am going.

I'm going to town tonight to take Aunt Maude up on an offer to use her bathtub. We have only cold showers and it is hard to

Tent City life.

get clean under them. I am also going to buy my supper. Our chow isn't so good now and we don't get very much out here for some reason or other.

I'm getting a nice even brown color from the sun and I suppose some dirt also, well, anyhow I'm really "in the pink" of condition and can't complain very much. We've been doing "yardbird" work for the last few days. Sure does not work very hard as there are so many fellows that each one has little to do himself. We just have to keep moving all the time. They don't want us to lay around all day. *Thousands* of soldiers here in "Tent City." Guess that is all for now.

Love, Bob

———

February 28, 1943

Dear folks:

Another week has now gone by and today is a great day for us. It's payday! We are waiting to get our call from the paymaster, now.

I went to a dance last night at a Service Center on St. Petersburg's million-dollar pier. I went with my friend, Jerry Gredler. While there I wrote a letter to Barbara and I mailed some others, including one to you and to Bob Ames.

I will probably eat dinner this evening with Grandma, Uncle John and Aunt Maude.

I feel perfect, look good (so they tell me) and am happy, so you see everything is O.K.

Boy! When I do get home it's really going to be a strain on the ration book, because how I would like to eat one of your *swell* meals, Mom. *Oh boy!*

I still have plenty of money and will really be O.K. when I get my pay.

The weather is swell. A little cool at night, but I can really make a bed, now, to keep plenty warm in.

"Red" Clemons is going to let me use his camera if I want to, or else I am going to get some prints from him that he took of the gang in our tent.

A couple of tents are quarantined with measles. There still is too much dirt here, and yet I feel swell. I guess that's about all the news for today, so I'll give up about here.

Love, Bob

.————.

Letter Sent to Hotel to John, Maude and Grandma,
March 1, 1943

Dear folks:

I just received my alert orders, so I cannot have a pass tonight. I probably will be shipped tomorrow, so the chances are against my seeing you again before I leave. However, I may be sent to town for a day or two before I leave Florida so I may get to see you once again before I leave. However, I doubt it. I am going to destination 287 wherever that is.

If I get a chance to call or come to see you before I leave, I certainly will try my best to get in to see you but the passes are pulled for all of us who are leaving so the chances do not look so good.

"Red" said he would bring this letter to you so you'll know what's what.

In case I don't get to see you again, I want to *thank* you ever so much for everything you have done for me. *Thanks a million!*

Well I'm glad I can get on to school but I really had a good time down here and consider myself very lucky to have been sent here.

I will let you know where I am stationed just as soon as I am able to. Maybe I'll beat you home, Grandma, wouldn't that be something?

You understand that I am on an "alert" which means that I probably will go in the next 2 or 3 days. I thought I would write this note now, because I will get no more passes from here so far as I can find out. May leave tomorrow.

I'll try to let you know just when I am leaving, but this is probably as close as I can get to that time. Thanks for everything, and I'll hope to get to see you before I leave.

Love, Bob

.————.

CHAPTER 4

ST. PETERSBURG, FLORIDA

Dearmont Hotel
March 3, 1943

Dear Dad, Mom and Kath:

Goodbye St. Petersburg? Here I come! By the time you get this I will be far from here. I got my final "alert" notice, Monday, and my shipping orders, yesterday. Right now I am in the Dearmont Hotel in St. Petersburg. We left "Tent City" at 9:15 this morning. I just had a swell bath here in town and do I feel good!

So far as I know now both Jerry Gredler and I are going to the same destination number, but we can never tell. I can't get out to see Grandma and the others, but "Red" Clemons took them a note from me Monday evening.

I guess I am leaving here in the morning so I suppose the next letter you get from me will be from my new home for a few months.

Boy, did it ever storm last night, but our tent was pretty good and I didn't get wet at all.

I got two letters from you yesterday and also the "greetings from Madison" folder. *Thanks a lot.* I can even see the Gay Building in a couple of the pictures.

As to my stay in St. Petersburg, I can honestly say I have had a good time, good training and good luck. I really feel wonderful (in spite of poor food now and then) and if I have as nice a place to go to school in, I will consider myself an *extra* lucky guy.

I sure would like to see you and "Bobbie" (Barbara) but your letters make up for a lot. I'm having lots of fun and am with a swell group of fellows.

Lots of love,

Bob.

———

Note from Mom

Left St. Petersburg at 7:30 p.m. Friday March 5, on troop train. Called us from Stevens Hotel, Chicago on Sunday eve, about 6:30.

Excerpt from a Letter from Grandma Gay Written March 6, 1943

Thursday eve. Bob called up and said they would leave Friday at 4:30. We all watched for a special train on the R.R. across from our hotel—no sign of a train, so Maude and I went up to the other depot which is 8 or 9 blocks from here—no trains leaving from there.

By the time we got back here, we were warm and tired. After we had supper, some were sitting outside, Maude & I were in. John came in. "Come quick a troop train is going to pull out ahead of the 7:30." Everyone who knew Bob made a run to get out on the side where the trains pass, and there was Bob with his face to the window. Maude & I threw kisses & he returned them so we knew he saw us. About 25 or 30 of us out there.

CHAPTER 5

CHICAGO, ILLINOIS

March 8, 1943

Dear Pop, Mom and Kath:

As you can see, I have a new address!

Well, I'm sure now that I am a lucky guy. Here I am in the largest hotel in the world. It is really swell here and I do mean *swell*! The hotel has all its rugs in it and dressers, writing tables, chairs, lamps, etc. All the same as it was before the army got it, except for the large beds etc. We have swell beds, though, clean sheets, blanket, comforter, pillows, and pillow case. We ride elevators all the time, too. Boy is it swell! Fourteen elevators and twenty-five floors. I am only on the sixth floor. We eat *wonderful* food in the large dining room. The coffee shoppe downstairs is still open and we can buy meals, pie, ice cream etc., just as people did before. Lots of telephones, a telegraph office, two post exchanges, large lounge (also one on each floor), an eye doctor and just about everything. Boy, is this a layout. It is supposed to be the best place to stay of any post in the whole country and *it is*!!

Chicago is also rated as first for its service to servicemen. Wonderful Service Center where we can eat, dance, play pool, get free tickets to all the shows in town, etc. We can even ride the busses and street cars free. Boy is this ever a swell place. You have to admit that I have been awfully lucky. I even had a much better and longer basic training than the majority of fellows here did. We got about the toughest training the Air Corps gives, but I'm awfully glad we had it.

We eat anytime we want to during certain hours. Boy, will I ever gain weight, here. We get about all the milk, butter and sugar we want. The food is actually swell! Civilian cooks and other help. We don't have to do any K.P., guard duty, or detail work while going to school.

This is a school for radio operators and mechanics, combined. In Madison, they get either radio operator or mechanics, but I will get them both. Isn't that swell? Boy, am I glad that I was on the ball when I took those tests before I was classified. Now it is paying off.

I will be in school for eighteen weeks here. After I complete the course, I will be shipped to a new destination immediately. Then we are supposed to get a fifteen-day furlough. Maybe we won't get it, but we are supposed to get one then. We can't get it until we arrive at wherever we are sent. We got this information this a.m. from an officer. Pretty nice, huh?

I'm going to study plenty hard, because this is a chance millions of boys would give a lot to have, so I've just got to make *good*!!

We don't know just when we will start school, but it will probably be this week. I am anxious to get going on it.

There are only three of us in the room, and is it ever nice; one double bunk, one steel cot, two lamps, one easy chair, one desk, one full length mirror, one large dresser, one glass top writing table, swell bath room, etc. *Really style!!* The Air Corps is really *the* place. I can see that now.

We are supposed to get passes soon. They are good within thirty miles radius of Chicago. However, the corporal told me that I might be able to get a special pass to come home sometime on my day off. I sure hope I can!

We go to school six days a week. I do not know what shift I will be on yet. There are three shifts. Anyhow we get about thirty-six hours off each week. I don't know what day this will be on yet, but I will let you know as soon as I can.

Robert Gay Glad He's in Air Corps

Pvt. Robert L. Gay, son of Mr. and Mrs. Len R. Gay, 702 Baltzell st., is mighty happy that he is one of the army air forces radio trainees living at the Stevens hotel in Chicago. He wrote his parents:

"I'm sure now that I am a lucky guy. Here I am in the largest hotel in the world, and it is almost the same as it was before the army took over. We ride elevators all the time. Boy is it swell! 14 elevators and 25 floors. I'm only on the sixth floor.

"We eat wonderful food in the large hotel dining room. The Coffee Shoppe downstairs is still open and we can buy food there just as people did before the army took over. There are lots of telephones, a telegraph office, two post exchanges, large lounge on every floor, an eye doctor, and just about everything. Boy, is this a layout. It is supposed to be the best place to stay of any post in the whole country, and I really believe it is.

"I'll probably gain weight here because we get about all the milk, butter, and sugar we want. The food is actually swell. They have civilian cooks and other help, so we don't have to do any K. P. guard duty, or detail work while going to school.

"There are three of us living in this room and is it ever nice. We have a double bunk, a steel cot, two lamps, an easy chair, a desk, a large dresser, private bath, and everything — real style! The air corps is really 'the' place, I can see that now.

"I feel swell and I'm sure happy. Am going to study plenty hard because this is a chance millions of fellows would give a lot to have so I've just got to make good."

* * *

Pvt. Robert L. Gay, son of Mr. and Mrs. Len Gay, 702 Baltzell st., considers himself the luckiest man in the world to be in the army air corps and to be stationed at the Stevens hotel in Chicago.

In a recent letter to his parents, Pvt. Gay, who will be in the Chicago training school for 18 weeks, told of his experiences at the school.

"Well, I'm sure now that I am lucky, he wrote. "Here I am in the largest hotel in the world. It is really swell here and I do mean swell! We have swell beds and wonderful food. Chicago is rated as first for its service to service men. There are wonderful service centers here, where we can eat, dance, play pool, get free tickets to all the shows in town and free transportation on the busses and street cars. I feel swell and I'm sure happy. I consider myself the luckiest guy there is."

Pvt. Gay said that he had "about the toughest training course that the air corps gives," but added that he was glad he had it.

Pvt. Gay will receive training both as a radio operator and as a radio mechanic.

"I'm going to study plenty hard," he said. "Because this is a chance millions of boys would give a lot to have. So I've just got to make good."

* * *

Wisconsin State Journal article.

I feel swell, and I am sure happy. I also consider myself about the luckiest guy there is. I sure hope I can see you soon. I'd sure like that. I guess that's all for now.

Love, Bob

Say, Pop, what about my income tax? Do I have to file a report or should I forget it for now?

•———•

March 10, 1943

Dear Pop, Mom and Kath:

Do I feel swell! Wow!! I am now a private first class, out of that "buck private" class at last! I guess it isn't so much, but it is a start and I get four bucks more each month. If you need any cash, Pop, just drop me a line. I lend to you on your signature only. Boy, doesn't that sound good? I even splurged and got a nice new G.I. haircut, really neat one as you will see. The fellows tell me that I will be able to get a special pass to come home on my day off, whenever that is. They say that I will be able to get one "sometime" so I don't know just how soon it will be, but I'll be home the first chance I get.

Mom, you should see the swell food we get here. For instance, today we had: Breakfast—bread, toast, butter, oatmeal, milk, scrambled eggs, bacon, strawberry jam and coffee for those who wanted it. For dinner—baked ham, potatoes, boiled cabbage, cabbage salad, tea, lemon pie, soup, crackers, 2 kinds of bread, butter and water. We get meals like these all the time, here, and you will have to admit they aren't bad, are they? Of course they aren't as good as your meals, but they are the next thing.

I sure hope you are all well and getting fat like me. If I don't get some exercise again soon, I'll be pretty heavy because I eat like a horse.

Well, I guess there isn't much more to tell today, so I'll let this letter drop six floors in a mail tube and get on its way.

Love, Bob

•———•

March 12, 1943

Dear folks:

I'm getting anxious to get started in school. I start at four tomorrow afternoon and go until 11:30 or 12 p.m. Then we have to sleep for eight hours, and then we can have a pass for a few hours during the day. That is how the situation stands at present, so far as I know. I believe that Saturday will be my day off but I'm not sure about that either. I guess I would just as soon have my undershorts sent down, if you think they are any good, but if not don't bother to buy new ones, because I can get them here if I need them. I got my laundry back today so I do not need the things so much. Also please do not send my radio as it is in a much safer place right now. Thanks ever so much for thinking of it.

I was made a PFC before I left St. Pete, but I didn't know it until we were on the train and the sarg. told us. However I didn't say anything about it until I knew for sure. We were made PFCs for the reason that we made this school and it was under the same order as at Truax Field, just as in the clipping. They just jumped the gun for us a little, I guess. Anyhow, it's swell and I like it here fine.

Love, Bob

·———·

March 16, 1943

My room number has been changed to 733, promoted to one floor up, ha ha.

Dear folks:

I got a letter from Uncle Rob inviting me to eat with him anytime that I can.

I am *really* busy now and I'm not fooling either. I get up at 8 a.m., eat breakfast after roll call and then clean up the room. Then we have a little time in which to study (if we get our rooms cleaned fast enough). At 11:40 we fall out for calisthenics and drill which lasts until 1 or 1:30 p.m. We fall out again at 2:40 p.m. for dinner, after which we go to the Congress Hotel for our radio mechanics class. The mechanics class is from 3:40 p.m. until 7:00 p.m. We eat supper at the Congress and then march about one mile to the Colosseum for radio code, which lasts from 8 p.m. to 11:40 p.m. Now here is where our free time comes in. It is about 11:45 p.m. when we get back to the hotel and if we want to we can go out from then until 1 a.m. However we must put on our class A uniforms, so that leaves about one hour that we may go out. So we just forget the passes and go to bed.

I believe we will have more free time after the first of April as they are going to change the school hours. Anyway I get a whole day off each week. From 11:40 Thursday p.m. until 2 a.m. Saturday. Those are the hours I am off duty. If I can get a special pass to come home, I will also get a few more hours to stay.

School is tough but very interesting and I like it a lot.

Hope to see you before long.

Love, Bob

•———————•

March 18, 1943

Dear folks:

Thank you for sending me the check. I am down to where I can really use it. This getting settled in the army costs a little, at that. I have had to buy socks, undershorts, chevrons, etc. Anyhow, I'm pretty well set now. I'll send the money back when I get paid at the end of the month.

I had hoped I would get home tomorrow, but I won't be able to make it. Better luck next time! I hope!!

I certainly am sorry to hear about Bob Bjerk. He was a *swell guy*. He was engaged, I believe.

I am sorry I couldn't get home, yesterday, but I have hopes for next week.

I feel swell and like school very much, but it is ever tough. I'm getting along swell, so far. I especially like the operators course, but the mechanics course is really something too. I'll bet Pop would like the mechanics course, because he likes that sort of a thing so well. We are learning about transformers, resistors, volts, amps, ohms, volt, amp and ohm meters, etc.

I'll call soon, when I get a chance. You can send me my "Buddy" Book that Uncle Alvin gave me for Christmas now, Mom. I'll have to get some transfer dates, etc. in it before I forget them. You can also send my undershorts, undershirts (including the sleeveless ones). Say hello to everyone for me, as I have very little time to write.

I hope you are all as well as I am, that's *perfect*.

Love, Bob

.———.

NOTES FROM MOM

SUNDAY A.M.

Bob phoned and told us what a grand visit he had with Bud, etc. Also that he had his first test, yesterday, in mechanics and got 100. Was he ever happy. Dad asked him if he was having fun. He said, "I sure am." We told him to wire us if he could get a pass to come home, if not we would be down there, at the Palmer House at 11 o'clock Friday, to spend the day and night with him, until he goes back at 2 o'clock.

MARCH 26, 1943

Kathryn, Dad and I took the 7 o'clock train to Chicago to spend the day with Bob.

He met us at the Palmer House at 11 o'clock.

We took the birthday cake, which Grandma Lee baked and brought in. Celebrated Bob and Kathryn's birthday in our hotel room on the 23rd floor #2337 W., eating cake.

We took Eugene Sasman's picture with us and had it standing on the dresser all p.m. and evening.

Dad walked back to the post with Bob at 10:40 p.m. Bob took leftover cake & box of cookies, which Grandma Lee sent to him, to his room.

.———.

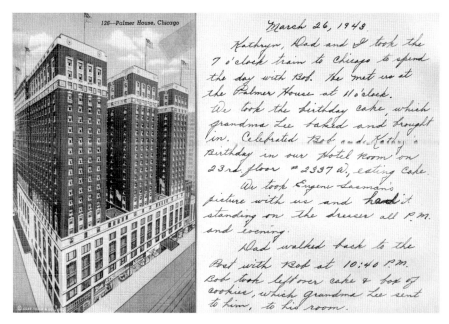

March 26, 1943.

Kathryn, Dad and I took the 7 o'clock train to Chicago to spend the day with Bob. He met us at the Palmer House at 11 o'clock.

We took the birthday cake, which grandma Lee baked and brought in. Celebrated Bob and Kathy's Birthday in our Hotel Room on 23rd floor #2337 W, eating Cake.

We took Eugene Sasman's picture with us and had it standing on the dresser all P.M. and evening.

Dad walked back to the Post with Bob at 10:40 P.M. Bob took leftover cake & box of cookies, which grandma Lee sent to him, to his room.

Chicago's Palmer House, where Bob had a visit with his family near his birthday.

Bob with his mom during one of her visits to Chicago.

April 12, 1943

Dear folks:

Right here I want to wish Pop a *very, very happy birthday*. I have a present coming for you, Pop, but it won't be there for your birthday I am sorry to say. It will come before long.

Mom, I want to thank you for fixing everything up so extra swell. Thanks a million. *You are wonderful!* It will be good to see you Friday. We will all have a swell time, I know. I will come out to Uncle Alvin's just as early as I can Friday morning, and if it is O.K. with you I thought that Bobbie and I would come into town after lunch and then come back late Friday night. O.K.? It will really be swell. I may get a few extra hours off, but that remains to be seen.

My cold is much better today. I doped up with Vicks last night and it helped a lot. I am sure I will be all better before Friday.

How is Yippee? I sure miss the little pup.

When are you coming down again, Pop? Let me know the next time and we will make a day of it. We'll have to hunt up a fire-boat or something. Bob Sasman and I were around the river, but we couldn't find it. If you let me know when you are coming I'll meet you by myself and we will have a good time together. Frank and I both had a swell time the last time you were here.

I will write again soon. Happy Birthday on the 14th, Pop, and have many, many more.

Love, Bob

.———.

Notes from Mom

April 16, 1943
Well, Kath, Barbara and I got down there, but Bob's pass was pulled & he was to be shipped, so we only saw him at the post.

April 17, 1943
Bob was shipped from Chicago to Truax Field via Chicago, Milwaukee, & St Pete R.R. arriving in Madison at 9:30 p.m.

Letter from the chaplain to Bob's dad.

Bob with Kath when she graduated from high school.

AUTHOR'S NOTE

There would be no letters home during Bob's time at Truax. He was a Madison boy in his hometown, and his family and friends kept him busy every chance they got. He and his friends were often spoiled with home-cooked meals, etc.—and Bob took delight in showing off his favorite things about Madison. He got to visit his family home sixty-four times during this period from April 17 to September 15 and was even there for his sister Kath's high school graduation.

NOTE FROM MOM

He graduated from Radio Mechanics & Electronics on Sept 7.
   He then had 48 hours leave from the Seventh at noon until the 9th at noon.
   He shipped from Truax on September 15.

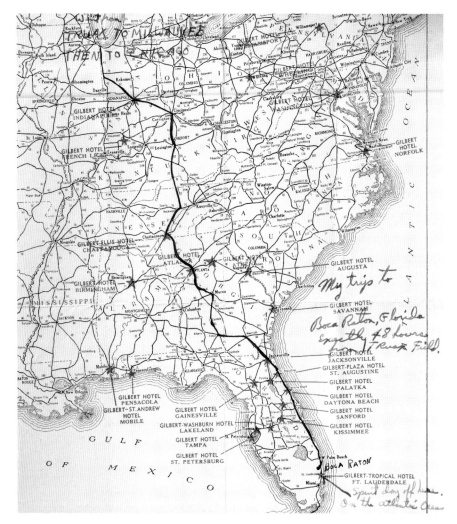

Bob's trip from Chicago to Boca Raton.

BOCA RATON, FLORIDA

Card
September 16, 1943

Dear folks:

Left Truax at 5 p.m. yesterday. Did not go through Madison. Went to Milwaukee, Chicago, Indianapolis and pulled into Cincinnati, Ohio at 7 a.m. today. Will arrive in Chattanooga, Tenn. at 5:15 today. It is now 4:30 p.m. Riding in Pullman. Excuse scribble, but train is swaying. All is fine.

Love, Bob

•———•

September 20, 1943

Dear folks:

I just got back from chow and will now drop you a cheerful note from beautiful and *darn hot* Florida. I haven't found a single person as yet who likes it here. It is hot, and when I say <u>hot</u> I really mean it. Temperature is over 95 degrees in the barracks most of the day. Nights are not so bad.

I went to school last night and it seems to be a better school than Truax so far as equipment and teaching methods are

One of the many telegrams Bob sent home.

concerned. I really do not know how I will make out. Only time will tell! It may not be such a long time before I will know whether I will make it or not. It is really tough. Many of the boys that I knew up there are already washed out. I'll just try to do it so that is that for the present.

There are many interesting things around here that I would like to tell you about, but we are not allowed to write about them.

The boy next to me happened to see my name when I moved in and asked if I was related to Dr. Gay in Chicago. He lives in Chicago and went to Uncle Rob 6 years ago for treatments.

If anyone ever wants to know what I am doing just say that I am at an *advanced radio school*. Not what we mentioned at home. You know what I mean—Army restrictions, etc.

After sampling a few more meals, we have decided they were better at Truax. It seems as if everyone's ambition, here, is to leave. A good ambition at that.

I have never seen so many mosquitoes in one spot in my life. All kinds of bugs here. I am already getting used to them however, so it's O.K.

I feel swell and everything is going on in regular Air Force style. Kind of crazy at that. I should have a good tan very soon.

Good night,

Love, Bob

·———·

September 22, 1943

Dear folks:

Today has been an extra busy one, as we have to wear our gas masks at all times from 8 a.m. to 5 p.m. I only had to wear mine from 12 noon until 5 p.m., because I sleep until noon on this shift. Every now and then they would turn tear gas loose at us and into the masks we would go. On the way to chow a regular truck started to pass the formation and all of a sudden they let us have it through a jet in the side of the truck. It's *nice stuff*. We got it now and then during the day, but I was quick enough with my mask so I didn't get much.

Boy a fellow sure should be in good shape when he leaves here. They give us a workout such as the gang will never forget.

I have a wonderful sunburn on my nose, shoulders, back, legs and arms. Generally all over, I guess. It feels warm, but not sore.

There isn't much news to write about. We have a lot of fun teasing the girls in the P.X. about being "rebels," also about their accents. Boy, they really take a lot of razing from us. They seem to get a kick out of it too, so I guess they don't get too mad. Most of them are married to permanent party men here. We just tease them to have something to do besides eat over there. Chow here isn't so good but we do eat. The P.X. comes in handy for lunches between meals. It is usually packed. A fellow gets plenty hungry around here, but I guess it won't hurt me any.

I am still plugging along in school. I don't know how well I am doing, but I am having a hard time of it.

The sky at night around here has more stars than I have ever seen. Literally millions of them. Very pretty.

Hope I get a letter tomorrow.

Love, Bob

·———·

September 26, 1943

Dear folks:

I am now in a very nice Service Center in Fort Lauderdale. A boy in my barracks named Gilbert Feeg and I came in last night by bus, around 7:30 p.m. He was in my class 12 at Truax and was an honor student. He is a very nice fellow.

We walked around for a while last night and took a room in a hotel for $1.50 each. It had two good beds but no bath. We then took in a show before we went to bed. This morning we got up at about 10:30 and have walked literally all over the town. Gil has his camera and a colored film so we walked all over so he could get some pictures. It costs a lot for most everything, down here, especially for meals.

I am very sorry to report that I am now eliminated from this school. I tried to get it but I just missed. I have quite a few fellows to keep me company, though. Of twenty-six in the class, sixteen of us washed out. They told us that we shouldn't feel bad about it because it is no shame to wash out here. Well over half do. I'm sorry, because I would have liked to have made it, but it may have its advantages too as many of the graduates are here for weeks and months before they ship out and even then get a raw deal. I still wish I could have made it though but I didn't, so that's that.

I am still attached to Truax. We all are for the first two weeks of school. It is now just a matter of waiting until Truax decides where to send me. They may ship me out on the line or back to Truax to take either CNS or a factory inspector's course. We'll just have to wait and see. I will be glad to ship out of here, that's for sure, as no one likes it at Boca Raton.

Everyone here is supposed to get advanced training before they leave here. It is really an intensified basic training which lasts four weeks, unless a fellow gets on a shipping order before he is started or during his advanced training. I hope I get my shipping orders *soon*!! We'll soon know.

Love, Bob

.————.

PHONE 2626

I ate here Sept 26, 1943 at 1:30 P.m. with Gilbert Feeg of Redding Penn.

OVERSEAS

A Restaurant of Merit

Marine Cocktail Lounge

Very nice Restaurant

215 S. ANDREWS AVE.   FT. LAUDERDALE, FLA.

From a day out in Fort Lauderdale with Gilbert Feeg.

September 28, 1943

Dear folks:

Well I just got off K.P. and am kind of tired, altho it was the easiest K.P. I have ever had.

I have been very busy the last couple of days. We worked all day yesterday and today. I will sure be glad when I get my shipping orders.

Today, I saw a plane crash about three blocks from my barracks. I was on K.P. yet and had gone outside for some brooms and another fellow and I stood for a minute to watch a formation of 6 P-40s (pursuit fighter planes—single seaters) flying over us about 1,000 feet heading for the field.

Suddenly one plane nosed up, hitting the tail of another just over us.

It made a loud crack and tore most of the tail off the one. The pilot gave it the gun, pointed it up and away from the barracks and then jumped. His chute just opened in time, because he was pretty low by then. His plane crashed right in the middle of the road three blocks from my squadron and barracks. It exploded and when I got there it was just a heap of junk. The pilot was there folding up his chute. He was kind of white and shaky, but I don't blame him. He did a good job getting away from the barracks like he did. The other plane that hit him just wrecked his propeller and made a landing on the flying field O.K.

There are crack-ups once in a while, but they sure keep them quiet because they don't even get into the papers. That junk pile, just a few minutes before, had been worth around $70,000. No one was hurt just added a little excitement for the day.

The engine went into the ground approx. 5 feet away at the edge of the road. I saw one radio tube laying a few feet away and it wasn't broken. Think of that!! The area was quickly roped off and guards kept the fellows quite a distance away. I supposed they had to make some investigations, etc.

I'll write again soon!!

Love Bob

P.S. I'm afraid I'll need some money, as we are not getting paid on the 30th. Could I please have about $10.00, money order is best. Thanks so much. I am sorry I had to ask for it, but I really need it down here. Everything costs about double what it should, even at the P.X. you pay plenty. I have spent some money on ice cream, cakes and milk especially. It is so hot here that we get awfully thirsty for something cold, and the water is far from cold, so we buy cold drinks. We got here too late to sign the pay-roll, thus we didn't get paid. We are apt to get shipped again before we are paid. I hated to ask for it, but Pop told me I should not go around broke.

.———.

Western Union Telegram
September 30, 1943

PLEASE WIRE 10 DOLLARS LOVE = BOB

.———.

Author's Note

His dad sent twenty dollars.

·———·

October 3, 1943

Dear Mom, Pop and Kath:

Well, I'm now in real training again. This training which I am now starting is supposed to be similar to that of the Infantry. I have moved up into the far north area of the camp to take A.T. (advanced and intensified training). We will spend lots of time on the gun range, lectures and close order drill, also we are to get in some 20-to-25-mile hikes with full pack. Later they give water safety.

Some fun, eh? However, I am pretty sure I will be shipped before I get much of this training.

Where I am now situated there are thousands of nice little sand fleas, and boy, do they ever bite! Wow!

Tomorrow I have to take an examination for air crew member. It will probably tell the story as to whether I will fly in the Army or stay on the ground crew. I hope I pass it O.K., but I am afraid my eyes and height will keep me off the planes.

I'll write tomorrow if I can. Goodnight,

Love, Bob

·———·

October 5, 1943

Dear folks:

As I told you before, I believe, I am now in advanced training unit. It isn't so easy up here as it has been in the past. We drill close order and extended order, have two to three hours of good stiff calijumpics (calisthenics) plus range, etc. We are on the go for ten hours a day at least. They take roll call about seven times a day to see if we are still with them, I guess. We are all hoping for our shipping orders to come through very soon.

I hope I get back there soon enough to see the Kimballs, if they come. It seems as if about 80% of the washouts are going back to Truax. I imagine I will have a pretty good chance at that rate. I did not pass my aerial gunners exam because of my eyes and my height. I would have liked to have passed it, but it can't be helped.

Noon 12 p.m.—a.m.—Just Noon!!

It is now noon and I have just eaten a meal with relish, because I was so hungry. The meal was so poor that I wouldn't have fed it to Yippee for $10, however, I ate it because I was darned hungry and had to eat something. I still feel good though so I imagine I will live through it O.K.

We spent the whole morning learning about the U.S. Army carbine rifle. It is really a honey. This afternoon we will learn to take it apart and put it together, etc. The next two days we will spend on the range firing the carbine and the machine gun.

Take it easy. I feel fine and hope you do, too.

All for now, love,

Bob

.————.

October 7, 1943

Dear folks:

Maybe they will let us be, long enough for me to get a letter off to you.

We have been plenty busy lately. We get up at 5:15 a.m. and keep on the go until 5:00 p.m. At 5:30 we have chow and then mail call at 6:00 p.m.

The day before yesterday our barracks was "gigged." We had to go out and drill an hour, from 6:30 to 7:30 p.m. that night.

The last two days we have been on the range and did a lot of shooting; really did do quite a bit of shooting. I really did do O.K., too, even if I do say so myself. We learned to field strip (take apart and assemble) the U.S. Army carbine cal. 30 rifle and the Thompson M1A submachine gun cal. 45. We really had fun on the range guessing as to how we would make out.

I got a "sharpshooter" rating with the carbine and an "expert" rating with the submachine gun. I'll get some medals, now! Here are the different ratings that are possible to get: starting with the lowest first. First comes "qualification," then "marksman," next to best "sharpshooter" and best "expert." I liked it especially well here, because it was impossible for anyone to cheat like was frequently done at Truax with the "pistol." Whatever a fellow earns here, he earned truthfully! After I had done my shooting I worked in the "pit." It is like being in a trench because the bullets whined overhead—pretty neat. It isn't unsafe there, though.

I'm sure glad I did O.K. These are the two main weapons used in jungle warfare, especially by Air Corps personnel.

Will write more when I can.

Love, Bob

.————.

October 11, 1943

Dear folks:

Saturday night came along so I headed to the 636th Orderly Room for my pass. I thought I was going to Miami, but my pass got mixed up and was made out for Palm Beach, so off I went. I went by myself and later that night I met Koelbl in a restaurant there. I got hungry about 10 p.m. and just happened to pick the right eat house.

It took me about one hour and twenty minutes to get there from Boca Raton. I looked around for quite a while for a room and finally found one in the Hotel Dixie Court. I then walked around, went to a show and then I met Koelbl. We looked around town and ate about five times before we went to the hotel.

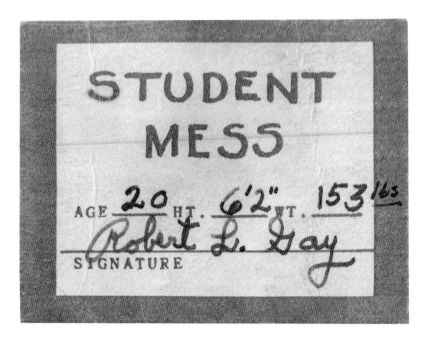

Bob's student mess card.

Bob's tech school ID.

Sunday morning I got up about 11 a.m. and checked out. We looked the town over by day light and found it to be a very nice town. I took a few pictures with the camera which Aunt Maude sent me. I hope they turn out O.K. It happened that the sky was cloudy around the early part of the afternoon, thus I didn't get any Florida sunshine in the pictures.

Tomorrow we start our "water safety" phase of A.T.U. We learn how to jump 20 feet into the water with packs and clothes on, plus swimming with a rifle held out of the water and so on. It should be interesting.

We saw a lot of Royal Air Force men from England in Palm Beach; also French army officers, navy officers and sailors fighting for Free France. They wore the Cross of Lorraine, which is the symbol of the Fighting French Forces. It was interesting to see them and hear them talk. We got a kick out of the French sailors. They were having a swell time. Some of them just got here and they were amazed at the things in the stores and the food. They were about as happy as I was when I got my first bicycle from Pop. They all were eating ice cream cones. Some had one in each hand.

I got paid last week so I am O.K. Thanks to you folks. I'm sure glad I'm getting those bonds, because I am sure to have money to pay you back with. I'll be glad to get away from here though, because everything costs enormous prices. It cost about forty cents for a ham sandwich and a glass of milk.

I really feel swell and I am happy. I hope I either get shipped to Madison, or if not there I hope to go out on the line around New York, Washington D.C., California, Washington State or Alaska. How's that! O.K. I guess when we get right down to it, most any place will do. It will have to!

I guess that is all for now. Take care of yourselves.
Love, Bob

.———.

Bob with his pal Joe Koelbl in West Palm Beach, Florida.

Air-Mail
October 14, 1943

Dear folks:

As you, by now, should have guessed after receiving my wire to stop the paper, I am leaving here very soon. Better not write any more as I won't be here to get the letters. I won't mention the day I am leaving. It is the day that Kathryn could have the most time to ride horses if she wants to. Don't know where I will go for sure, but I think you have the best idea as to "where." I hope it is the right idea! All of us feel pretty happy today.

The last two days we have spent at "water safety," as Claude mentioned to you, Mom, at the beautiful Boca Raton Club. We swam, dove, jumped off a twenty-foot tower into fifteen feet of water with a pack, helmet and rifle. Quite a thrill!! I don't like swimming in salt water, though. Fresh water is lots better. I have a pretty fair tan now. Hope you can see it *soon*! We did not finish our water safety, had one more day to go, but we were moved back to our old 636th Squadron, from A.T.U.

I hope you all feel as swell as I do, especially *today*.

Hope to see you soon!

Love, Bob

•————•

Saturday, October 16, 1943

Dear folks:

I never did get to Miami and we are restricted this weekend so it doesn't look as if I'll make it. I got to see quite a bit around here nevertheless.

I have had fun here, as I always do wherever I go, but I have never been as happy to leave a place as I am to leave here. The others feel the same as I do. It is very hot today and I wish I had 100 lbs of ice to sit by for a while. Boy, oh boy! On the whole, though, the weather has been pretty good and the sky in Florida is really pretty, day or night. We can always see planes over here day or night. It is very interesting to see them go in and out of the clouds.

By the way, Pop, I'm no good at the galloping dominoes. I have learned my lesson on them, too. Cards and dice and I just don't get along so we stay away from each other from now on. I couldn't even qualify with them.

I feel swell, all of us feel especially happy now because of certain orders received.

All for now,

Love, Bob.

•———————•

CHAPTER 7
TRUAX FIELD, WISCONSIN

Note from Mom

October 22, 1943

Bob arrived at Truax after being in Boca Raton, Florida, for five weeks.

Began school, advance radio mechanics course called V.H.F. (very high frequency) on November 5, 1943–in 619th T.S.S.

Was home nearly every night for dinner until classes began. Began on night shift, having from Thursday at 11 o'clock to Friday at 1 o'clock off each week.

Elementary school #1006 burned to the ground on Friday, November 12 at 3:30 p.m. The army radio post's public relations office said the fire was restricted to the elementary radio classroom. No one was injured.

Bob graduated from V.H.F. course on December 17, 1943.

Was with us Xmas eve and then came out Xmas Day.

On January 3, 1944, was shipped to Salt Lake City with a delay en route.

He had a 10-day furlough on January 2 and was home from January 3 until January 14. Daddy & Mother went to Chicago on Friday the 14 to see him off for Salt Lake City.

CHAPTER 8

SALT LAKE CITY, UTAH

Postcard from Omaha Nebraska
January 15, 1944

Hi folks—
Am here for 15 min. Now 10:30 a.m. Friday morning. Met Boal
& Kelly at Chi just after you left. Swell trip so far.
Love, Bob

.———.

Postcard from Cheyenne Wyoming
January 15, 1944

8:45 p.m. mountain time. Am in this station. Have 15 min.
Having fun—hope you had a nice train ride Fri.
Love, Bob

.———.

Postcard from Ogden, Utah
January 16, 1944

Dear folks—
9:30 a.m. We are in Ogden for 30 minutes. Having fun. Seeing swell scenery but no pictures—as yet. Windows too dirty to take them thru! All for now.
Love, Bob

•————•

Headquarters Army Air Base
Salt Lake City, Utah
January 17, 1944

Dear folks—
Just a short while ago the train pulled into the siding and I found myself on the Army Air Base, Salt Lake City. It's a big place and plenty busy. It's part of the 18th Replacement Wing of Second Air Force. Nearly everyone assigned to Second Air Force passes through this base and after a few days here is assigned to a permanent Second Air Force Bomb Group or Air Base Squadron.

The chief reason that everyone comes through this station is to be processed. I have just finished processing, which means simply that I was paid in full, issued what clothing I needed, physically examined, and all my records were brought up to date. Now when I leave here and go to my permanent station I will have everything necessary and there will be nothing to interrupt my training.

I have been classified as radio mech., and in a few days will be off to my new assignment with the heavy bombardment airplanes which are a part of this Air Force.

I'll write again as soon as I can.
Love, Bob

P.S. Sent home camera. Finish film and develop, some pictures of Salt Lake City.

•————•

January 17, 1944

Dear folks:

Finally I have some time to get off a letter. I guess I will start my story from the time I saw you off from Chicago. O.K.? Well here goes—

I started to walk back to the Union Station to meet Gempler when his late train got in. About half the way over there I ran into Pat Kelly and Bob Boal, whom I have known since last August. They were going with us but I wasn't sure when they would get to Chicago. Well, anyway, we all headed back to the North Western Station again and there was Gempler. Boal and Gempler each got a seat, Kelly and I got berths just different cars but we spent the days and evenings together and really had fun. We spent a lot of time in the lounge car where we could get Cokes, lemonade and root beer.

We arrived here yesterday a.m. and went directly to the nearest U.S.O. so we could leave our baggage and look the city over. Most everything was closed but we did see quite a bit. We looked over the Mormon temple which was interesting to see and saw the capitol from the distance. I took some pictures of the Mormon temple and the fellows. I hope some of them are good. It was cloudy part of the time. There is a very large snow-capped mountain just in back of the white capitol building. It is really beautiful.

We came out to the base at 9:00 p.m. We were given two dirty blankets and put into the barracks for the night in the processing area. This a.m. we got up at 4:45 and ate breakfast after which we went to the processing building, and spent the day as follows: found barracks bags, had strict clothing check, hot shower (went through long hall full of showers, washing and rinsing on the way), had physical examination just like the one I took when inducted last year, then all of our records were brought up to date, service records, etc., checked dog tags to see if they were correct. We then had a short lecture on the 2nd Air Force and what will happen to us next. The government letter I sent today will explain quite a bit, but I will tell you what I know about it. It is a heavy bombardment force like is bombing Germany every day, Flying Fortresses, etc. Crews are made up here and sent out to train just as the ground forces are. Everyone here (there are many believe me!) is a specialist of some kind— radio, mechanic, pilot, navigator, gunner, bombardier, sight specialist, etc. I probably will be here from three to ten days, during which time we will be sent to some permanent squadron in the U.S. for combat training. This may last from two to six months. Probably will remain in same squadron for the duration. However will not necessarily be kept in 2nd Air Force. The whole squadron to which I will be assigned can and probably will be transferred to another Air Force.

I passed my physical examination O.K. today and got my classification as follows: Radio Mechanic—1A. Full Field— General Service— Fit for Overseas Duty. It doesn't look like I will go overseas for quite a few weeks at least so don't worry about me. Finally we were issued new equipment that we needed. I got new canteen and cover, leggings and a new raincoat. I signed statement of charges for canteen, cover and leggings.

I feel fine, the food is good. I have K.P. tomorrow a.m. at 3:45. Will all be glad to leave here for new base. Barracks nice but very crowded. Hope you are all fine and dandy.

P.S. Tell Ed and Connie the new portfolio works swell.

Take care of yourselves.

All my love, Bob

.———.

January 20, 1944

Dear folks:

Well, here I am again. Hope everyone is feeling fine today.

We were put on the "alert" this morning and will probably ship tomorrow to where I mentioned in yesterday's letter. We all have to take a short refresher course there.

Yesterday I saw a B-24 bomber come in on its nose. It has a tricycle landing gear. Well the nose wheel wouldn't come down. The pilot really did a swell job in landing. When the nose came down it slid along on the ice just as if it were on a ski. No one got hurt and all it did to the plane was chew up the nose a bit. I saw it in the hanger where I was working on a detail today. We worked "around" bombers, etc., just wiping up grease spots, etc. Not working on the radios, must wait to be assigned to permanent squadron before we can do that.

When I write again about tomorrow it will be from my new destination of which I am practically positive will be very close.

Love, Bob

•————•

CHAPTER 9

CAMP KEARNS, UTAH

Squadron B
18th Replacement Wing Det.
Camp Kearns, Utah
January 22, 1944

Dear folks:

I shipped from the Air Base to here this a.m. We will be here for a couple of weeks at least, I believe. We must take a six-day refresher course while here. Probably will not start school until next week, however will do detail work, K.P., etc. until then.

This base is not half as good as the one at Salt Lake City. We have barracks like Truax has. The camp is very large and spread out. Many different phases of war are carried on here. Every inch of ground is covered with about two inches of ice. We slid all over the place. We carried our barracks bags one mile today on the ice, more fun!! We are about 17 or 18 miles away from Salt Lake. Came in trucks today, no train for this long trip. Tsk-tsk!!

Oh yes, it's O.K. to write now as I'll probably be here long enough to get some letters. It will be very swell to get them, too! I want to hear how you all are.

Happy Birthday Mom.

All my love,

Bob

January 25, 1944

Dear Mom, Pop and Kath:

The everlasting fog and snow finally cleared up enough today so we could see a few miles. This place is a flat space located between two ridges or ranges of snowcapped mountains. The mountains are pretty but very poor in comparison with the beautiful ones we saw in Colorado on our trip west a few years ago. The field itself seems very dismal and poorly laid out. There is absolutely nothing to do but go to the show or sit on your bed during the evenings if you are fortunate enough to have a free evening. We are in good spirits, though, because we have fun just fooling around.

Mom, I hope you had a swell birthday. Don't think I have forgotten about it because I sure have not. Things here make it tough as far as presents are concerned. Here is an extra Happy Birthday for you until I can do better. I hope your cold and back are both all O.K., Mom. Take good care of yourself and don't work too hard, promise?

Love, Bob

·———·

January 27, 1944

Dear folks:

I hope that my luck holds out for a while now. Today is the first day they didn't get me on detail. It is really a treat. I took a swell shower last night and got dressed all up. Today I am over at the Service Club which is over one mile from my barracks. It is built similar to the ones at Truax but is not as nice. This field is really dead. There isn't anything to do at all. By popular vote among us veterans from Boca Raton, we have decided this is just a trifle worse than Boca.

We just gorged ourselves at lunch here. This is the first time I have been over to the Service Club. We had a good roast beef dinner. Plenty of cartwheels (silver dollars) here. Remember them? Few paper bills. I have plenty of money left so everything's

O.K. We probably will be paid in a couple of days so you can see that I'm fixed up O.K.

Is there much snow at home? Plenty around here. I sure would love to go skating some place. Don't think I am griping, folks, I am not. There will no doubt be many places far worse than this so everything is really O.K.

I hope to hear from you soon.

Love, Bob

.———.

January 30, 1944

Dear Mom, Pop and Kath:

It sounds as if you have been having a swell time, Mom. I'm glad, also happy to hear that you are feeling so well. It sounds as if Kath is keeping on the ball O.K. Am glad she did so well in school. I hope very much that she will keep it up. I want her to graduate from the U of W. I know she will not be sorry if she does. Keep it up, kid. It sounds awfully good to me. Have a good time, too. Don't forget!

I started school two days ago 8 a.m. and got out at 5 p.m. Have at least 4 more days to go if I pass all the sets. If I don't, I must go until I make the others O.K. It is really a tough brush-up course and I don't mean maybe! The guys still at Truax who think like I did, that their toughest schooling is over when they graduate, are sure going to have a surprise. I have gone to school here for two days and have completely covered five different sets. Have plenty more to go. There is so much to remember that if I can do it all… well, it will sure be swell.

I got a nice letter from Tom Jones at Camp Hale the other day. He said he was awfully glad that I went to see his folks while I was home. I am glad I did too.

I believe I will get a new shoulder patch soon. I read in the paper that the 2nd Air Force has got a new insignia, but it did not describe it. I have got a swell friend here. His name is John Copeland. He comes from Findelay, Ohio. He is a sgt., areal [*sic*] gunner and radio operator. All for now. Swell to hear from you.

Love, Bob

•———————•

February 1, 1944

Dear folks:

Hope you are all as fine as I am. I just got back from a half hour show. It was Les Brown and his orchestra in person. Pretty good show!

School is really going great guns. I have learned more in three days than I ever learned in three weeks before. This radio is something that no one can ever get through learning about, because there is always something new to study about.

I still have plenty of money, folks. Thanks for asking. I am glad to hear that you are having fun… going to shows, etc. Also that the weather, there, has shown you some nice days.

I have a terrific test coming up before long so I have to study tonight. It covers all the sets I have ever studied.

How is Yippee? Bye for now,

Love Bob

•———————•

February 9, 1944

Dear folks:

Here I am again, just got out of school and am taking it easy at the Service Club. What a life!

Yesterday morning when I got up there was no snow left on the ground. It started to snow and kept it up all day. Today, I walked about a mile to the "Club," up to my knees in snow. It sure is pretty around here now.

When we got home from the show last night about 10 p.m. five of us played tackle in the snow. Fine football weather. When we fell down it was like landing on a hay stack. I know it sounds crazy but we had more fun than we have had since we got here.

The lieutenant came in the barracks about 9:15 this morning and everyone was still asleep. He made us get up and have the barracks cleaned up in twenty minutes, then he put us on detail

Bob with his pal Dick at Kearns, Utah.

policing the area. He left in about ten minutes, then we all scattered. Tomorrow morning we will be up earlier.

I'm growing fat and lazy, now that school is over, here. I hope to get going soon. It will be a real surprise when I get to my next base because I have no idea as to where it will be. I am pretty sure I will go out in a civilian train. I hope so, because it is more fun than on a troop train.

I have read a few good books in the library here, to help pass the time away. This sitting around while waiting to ship is all right.

All for now, I guess.

Love, Bob

·————·

U.S.O. Postcard
February 12, 1944

Dear folks,

I finally got out of camp for a few hours. I am in Murry, Utah, about 8 miles from Camp Kearns. Came in with a truck caravan to a dance at this U.S.O. Am having a pretty good time. Came here at 7:30 p.m. and trucks will take us back at 12:30 p.m. tonite. All for now—

Love, Bob

P.S. Maybe I will get a chance to write again tomorrow. We will see. Have hunch I will be nearer home soon. Maybe I'm wrong though?

·————·

Postcard from Colton California
February 16, 1944

Dear folks,

We got into Colton at noon today and had to wait till tonite before taking a Greyhound bus to Blythe. Went into San

Bernadino for the afternoon. It is a very beautiful town. Cal. has Florida beat all to pieces, so far!!

    Love, Bob

.————.

Postcard from Indio, California
February 17, 1944

Dear folks,

    Am in Indio, Cal. Left Colton, Cal. at 10 a.m. today.

    Beautiful trip! Wish you were here. Will write details on arrival.

Very interesting. Having fun. Riding on Greyhound. All for now.

    Love, Bob

.————.

CHAPTER 10

BLYTHE ARMY AIR BASE, CALIFORNIA

Blythe Army Air Base, California
February 18, 1944

Dear folks:

    I left Kearns at 8:30 a.m. on Tuesday. We went by truck to Salt Lake City where we caught the Union Pacific "Challenger" for Los Angeles. We went southwest through Utah and through Los Vegas to Colton, California. We were supposed to take a Greyhound bus from Colton at 2:30 p.m., however we decided to go back to San Bernardino and look it over. It is only five miles from Colton. We did go there and I sent you some cards and a telegram from there. We went back to Colton to get a six o'clock bus, but couldn't get on, so we were stuck for the night. We split up (there were six radio mechanics and four switchboard operators) and were looking about Colton when we were told to report to the police station.

    Here is what happened: one of the boys was asked for his pass by an M.P. and as he didn't have one he was taken to the police station. They rounded up the rest of us and told us to stick together because we were all on one order. One man had the sheet with our orders on it so we had to stay with him. The orders were our pass. We went to a show together and then slept in a servicemen's dormitory. More fun!

We caught the 8:49 bus in the morning and stood up for 200 miles, didn't mind it though because we had a lot of fun. We got here about five p.m. yesterday and I and two others were assigned to the 34th Bomb Group—18th Bomb Squadron. We reported to our squadron and they told us that they had enough radio mechanics in this squadron so we will be transferred to another one in a day or two; therefore, please *do not write* to me at this return address as I will not get the letters, as I doubt if they will follow me as no records were made on us in this squadron because we are being transferred.

This base is *very* large and has a huge number of planes, most of them are B-24's. It takes about twenty minutes to get from here to the P.X. by bus. It is three miles to the P.X. and theatre. This is an all-flying field, not rows of barracks like Truax is. We are about one-and-one-half blocks from the "line" where the planes are parked. There are always dozens of them overhead. When I am set I will send for my camera. We are out in the desert of southern California. We can see lots of sand and brush for miles and miles, way off are some mountains. It is tiresome to look at and yet has its own beauty. Our barracks are pretty good. They are made of composition and are tan in color, matching the color of the sand perfectly. Today we just walked around and watched the planes, saw them loading the bombs and machine guns, etc. Very interesting to watch! The officers are swell. We eat from our mess kits in a fair mess hall. We dish up ourselves and can have all we want. The food is pretty good.

There is a small town of Blythe about seven miles from here but it looks pretty dull. We saw many tanks, trucks, etc. on maneuvers as we came on the bus.

I hear we can have one three day pass each month from here, but that we will work seven days per week otherwise. This place goes like mad twenty-four hours a day. If I ever get a three-day pass from here I'll go to Elsinore to see Aunt Ruth. Most everyone goes to Los Angeles from here when they get a three-day pass. It takes approximately one day each way. Better not say anything to Aunt Ruth about it because I may not get a chance to go there. We'll see!

If I go overseas from here, which is very possible, I believe India or China would be an excellent guess, at least I believe it will be in that territory. Time will tell.

Bob on base in Blythe, California.

The group adjudent's [*sic*] name is Robert S. Gay. I hear that he comes from Milwaukee, but am not sure. Coincidence, eh?

All my love, Bob.

.———————.

Western Union Telegram
February 23, 1943

DEAR FOLKS PLEASE DO NOT SEND CAMERA AND MONEY AS REQUESTED I MAY TRANSFER OR SHIP WAIT TILL YOU HEAR FROM ME AGAIN ALL IS OK LOVE = BOB

.———————.

February 23, 1944

Dear Mom, Pop and Kath:

Today is a cool, cloudy and rainy day, not nice at all.

First I want to explain about the night letter that I sent last night. A friend of mine who is a clerk and works in the orderly room told me that he saw my name on a list that was either to transfer out of this squadron or to ship off of this field; therefore, I sent the telegram for you to hold the money and camera so it won't be following me all over heck or be lost. If you have already sent it don't worry about it because it will get to me eventually, I believe. As soon as I found out the score around here I will let you know when and where to send the stuff. I am sorry to be causing so much trouble, Mom and Dad, but everything is kind of mixed up around here and we don't know what the score is.

I went to work last night at 7:30 p.m. on the "flight line." Spent most of the night making "pre-flights" on B-24s. A "pre-flight" is a complete check on all the radio sets and radio equipment in the bomber. Must see that all is working as it should. We go from one end of the plane to the other. First, I check the chart in the plane to see if the pilot or radio operator has listed anything as not working right, then I climb into the pilot's seat and flick certain switches on the panel which starts a small, gasoline-driven generator for power while plane is on the ground. There are, of course, many steps in this job which I am leaving out because it would be dry reading and take all day and a lot of paper to write it on. I then check the 274-N Command set by calling the control tower for a radio check. He lets me know if I am coming in clearly, etc., also call a ground station, etc. This is just a short glimpse of what I do. That was for one set only. There are quite a few different sets on the plane. We work on a certain number of planes. There is a million other jobs to be done. The "pre-flight checks" are the simplest and most done. There are 100-hour and 300-hour checks to be made on each plane once a day. Checks which involve much more work. All the equipment must be taken from the planes and cleaned, completely gone over for bad tubes, wiring, etc.

Last night's work went very well. I am getting along fine so far. I'm pretty long to be crawling around in the bombers all night though. They are big bombers but have a lot of stuff in them. We crawl around between the bombs in the bomb bay, and from the tail-gunners position clear up to the pilot's position and bombardier's compartment. We have a lot of fun laughing at each other when we bump our heads or make some other mistake. Last night I was standing in the navigator's compartment checking the radio compass, I finished and turned out the light and when I was hooking up a shelf I stepped just about two inches too far and dropped right out of the plane through the hole that the nose-wheel fits in when the plane is in the air. There I was sitting on the cement ramp! Was I ever surprised! I laughed until I nearly died at my stupidity. All I got was a skinned knee and a razzing from a couple of the boys. It sure was funny though. I wish you could have seen it.

I must go and get a typhus and a cholera shot now, so will halt this letter about here. I hope you are all fine. Please say "Hello" to everyone for me. Thank you.

Love, Bob

•———•

Bob in a bomber.

February 25, 1944

Dear folks:

How is everyone today? Good I hope! I feel swell but would love to see the sunshine again. I always thought the desert in Southern California was dry, but it has rained for three days straight now. I guess this is the liquid sunshine that Bob Hope talks about.

Here I am right on the job. I just finished making radio "pre-flights" on five bombers and am now back in the shack. I have a bit of time now so thought I would drop you a note.

We usually finish our "pre-flights" by 2:30 a.m. so we just sit around and listen to the radio until morning. Every morning around 5 o'clock Pacific time we pick up a short-wave propaganda talk, in English, direct from Tokyo, Japan. You should hear the lies they spread if you think the Germans tell big ones, Wow! Last night they were telling how loathsome the Americans are because they treat the negroes so terribly and yet make them fight on the front lines for us. On and on they talk... They call us every name they can without actually swearing.

Each night they have a new and fantastic tale to tell about us. Boy oh boy, I hope to get a chance to get a crack at those little rats! This broadcast we listen to comes directly from Tokyo. It is the real thing and not just a program from San Francisco. I sure would like to have a receiver like the one we listen to, after the war. It is a receiver from the plane. They cost a fortune each and are above the regular broadcast band. Wish you could see one, Pop. You would love it! We can pick up police calls, ships and planes all over the country.

I have only one shot to go now. It will make the 17th or 18th shot since I have been in the Air Corps. "They didn't tell me I would have so many shots or I just wouldn't have let them draft me," is quoted from a cartoon [I saw], but quite accurate at that. Shots don't worry me in the least any more. Just another G.I. requirement.

Better hold on to the camera for a while yet.

All for now, love,

Bob

·————·

February 28, 1944

Dear Mom, Pop and Kath:

This morning when I got up our latrine was locked as they were cleaning it, so I walked about half a block to the next one to wash. As I was washing someone tapped me on the back and yelled "Hello" at me. It was Dick Levenick. You know his folks I am sure, live on University Ave. and goes to our church. Boy, was it good to see someone I know. Wow! He is a bomb-sight maintenance man. He is in the same squadron as I am and stays in a barracks approximately half a block from mine. He looks swell and feels fine as far as I can see. It really was a surprise say nothing of the coincidence.

I start the new shift this noon and work until midnight, work twelve hours a day seven days a week. It's O.K. though because there is no place to go anyhow. They cut out all three day passes yesterday but it still is possible to get a three- or two-day pass. Will try to make Los Angeles on that if I get one. It takes about eight hours to get there from here.

I guess it will be O.K. to send my camera now as I think I'm set for a while anyway. I hope I can get a few nice shots around here.

My pal, Andy Ference, whom I have mentioned in letters from Kearns, and I are on the same shift again which is plenty O.K. Wow, what a swell day this one turned out to be!!

I'm all done with my shots now. They won't be giving me any more for quite a while. I got my last typhus yesterday and they tossed in a new smallpox vaccination for good measure. I didn't know I was due one until yesterday.

Besides our work we have been getting two hours per day of chemical warfare, gas, thermite and incendiary bombs, etc. Say Pop, when you send the camera as I asked for in this letter can you stick in an Esterbrook pen point #2556. This point is all shot. (Any size will do.)

Thanks a million for the swell letters and all the news.

All for now,

Love Bob

.————.

March 1, 1944

Dear Mom, Pop and Kath:

You said you were confused as to whether you should send my money by mail or telegraph. By now I expect you have had following letters from me explaining that it would be best to send it by mail. I'm sorry to have caused the mix-up, but this whole joint is mixed up and confused. Thanks very much for your suggestions about wiring for it Pop. The telegraph station here is almost three miles from me and hard for me to get to as it takes quite a bit of time to wait for a bus that goes by there. I haven't got the spare time and besides money orders sent here come only as far as the town of Blythe, about seven miles from here.

I got a dollar in your letter just as you said and one in Mom's. Thanks very much. I'm holding out pretty fair, haven't had a chance to spend any at all for four days now.

We are really working hard around here now. For the last couple of days we have worked on the planes from twelve to sixteen hours per day. By the time we are off we are so tired we hit the sack and when we wake up it is time to work again. We are getting some new planes now and that is why we are working so long. It takes time to get all of them in shape.

Boy, I sure wish you could see these planes, they sure are large; hold 2,643 gallons of gas, Pop. Quite a long drive if it were for the car, eh? Don't quote that figure in the wrong places as maybe I shouldn't write such figures. O.K.? Good.

From now on I hear they are not going to paint any of the planes. We got a bunch of new planes in here today. Some are painted that dark green and some are not painted, just shining silver aluminum. It takes 200 pounds of paint per ship. Adds approximately fifteen miles per hour without paint, so they say. I sure hope I can sneak in a picture of one of them after I get the camera. I'll always send the film home to be developed.

I sure sleep good. Wow! I just pass out when I hit the bunk and don't hardly move until time to go to work, People with insomnia or whatever they call it could find a sure cure here.

Well folks, thanks again for the money and have fun. I'm off to two hours of lectures on overseas censorship and intelligence. Bye for now.

Love, Bob

P.S. How is school coming, Kath? Good as ever, I hope.
P.S.S. I shave three times a week now, what a life! Wow!

·———·

March 3, 1944

Dear Mom, Pop and Kath:

Thanks a million for all of your swell letters. I get mail from at least one of you every day. You can't imagine how good it is to get letters from home.

Pop, I hope the Oil Board gets all fixed up O.K. soon. I am glad to hear that you have a man to help you with some of your office work. You work too darn hard and it will be good for you to have some help. You asked me if I would like to buy a jeep? Well, I have driven them quite a bit now, and they are swell little cars for what they are built for, however I will still stick to liking cars like the little red Ford.

It was swell of Aunt Dorothy to offer to visit me at Blythe, etc., but as you know it is impossible for me to get any time off. All I could possibly get is one day. I shall write her and explain. It would have been good to see her though.

I have been doing and seeing a lot here on the base. Have been very busy. I wish I could tell you all about it but it will have to wait. Plenty going on. I am still working twelve hours per day and am plenty tired at night. We get so darn hungry that we eat at least four meals per day at the mess hall. It is not that the meals are good but just because we are hungry. Two big events each day: mail call and chow.

Tonight and tomorrow night I must go to school, intelligence course and censorship. Next week we get five days of two-hour classes on camouflage.

Left: Air Corps insignia patch. *Right*: The Eighth Air Force insignia that Bob's mother put on all the scrapbooks she created of everything he sent home.

Pop, I sure hope next year I can be home and help you out. Boy, will that be swell!! I'm not a bit afraid of work, that is for sure! *You know* how good it will be to be home again. I'll add up those books for you all you want me to.

Enclosed you will find some literature they gave us. It may be of some value to you if and when I go overseas. I doubt very much if I will go over in the outfit I am now with, if or when they go. We are still listed as overages.

I really feel good and am happy so don't worry about anything. I'll write more tomorrow.

Love, Bob

•———•

March 5, 1944

Dear folks:

Another day, another pile of dough on the pay-roll!! I not only received that swell money order from Pop the other day but I got a swell surprise from Grandma Gay. She is sure good to me isn't she.

I am still working pretty hard and am rather tired at night, however, I honestly do feel fine and in general everything is O.K.

I'm all set again financially, thanks to you!! I signed the pay-roll today and will probably be paid about the 10th or 15th of this month. I shouldn't be bothering you for money for quite a while now. Thanks again!

I hope all of you are feeling good. The weather has been swell for the last few days, sunny and warm. Millions of stars at night and not even a W.A.C. to help us enjoy them! Tsk! Tsk! The W.A.C.s are way up at the other end of the field, miles or so from here. Not many good-looking ones anyway.

Enclosed is the heading from the Blythe Army Air Base's paper. Good for our scrap-book, Mom. O.K? I hope you received the pictures I returned to you.

I would sure love to eat one of your swell meals, Mom! Boy, you sure are the best cook in the world!!

Nothing new today, so I guess I had better get to bed. Another 4:30 a.m. to 5:30 p.m. day tomorrow. Goodnight and take care of yourselves.

Love, Bob

P.S. Is it still snowy etc. there? I suppose it is. You might say "Hello" to the Predeauxs for me if you see them.

All for now,

Love Bob THE DESERT KID??

·————·

March 8, 1944

Dear folks:

Thanks for everything. I got the camera, pen point and pictures. Your letters are swell! Also got the second money order, thanks so much. *Please* don't try to send me anything for my birthday.

You have been too swell to me already. I have sure received *much more* than I should ever have for a birthday. Just keep those swell letters coming, a letter each day is more important than anything I could think of. Looks like Madison isn't through with its soldiers yet.

I am awfully sorry to hear about Dr. Sullivan's son. I hope he is going to be O.K.

Pop, it sounds as if you were too good a member on the ration board. I hope you can get off it O.K. if you are behind in the office work. You have sure done a lot more than your share if you ask me. I can see no way that they can keep or make you stay. Hope all turns out O.K.

As we are now working on a different section of the field, and on a day shift, I've not heard any more Tokyo propaganda talks, Mom, if I hear any more I will send them to you.

Yes we can have laundry and dry-cleaning done here. Most everything I own is now in the laundry. It takes two to three weeks to get either back. Kath, keep up those swell letters. You and Mary Lou sure have a real time. I get a real laugh out of you kids. Glad to hear Stuart is home. Thank you again, Sis!

Those pictures of all of us and the one of Kath are really neat. I'm awfully glad you sent them, Mom. I'm putting them in my little case. All of you look swell in them!!! I think you and Kath look real cute, Mom. And Pop, well, I think it is about the greatest picture of you (outside of us in the uniforms) I've seen in quite a while. It sure is swell to have a picture of all of us together.

Weather here is really swell! I've got a real red face but it isn't very sore. Getting a nice tan!!

The P.X. is O.K., Mom, we can get about everything we need there, including haircuts.

I'm still working hard, but only nine or ten hours per day now. Not so bad. I feel very fine and am awfully glad you do too. Everything is fine!

Please forget about the birthday presents as I have already got them. Swell pictures, letters and money! What more could a fellow ever want??

Take care of yourselves and have fun! Thanks, with all my heart, for everything.

Love
Bob

.————.

March 12, 1944

Dear Mom, Pop and Kath:

I'm sorry I haven't written for a couple of days but haven't had much of a chance. Besides work we are getting more schooling of one kind or another, such as map reading, airport camouflage, personal camouflage, aerial photographs, and more practice on the machine gun. You can readily see that I have managed to keep doing a little to keep busy. I did get to see a very, very good show the other day, it was "See Here, Private Hargrave." See it, by all means, if you can! It was really good.

Thanks for the fine letters. Got one from each of you and also one from Jerry which I am enclosing to you. Mom, thanks so much for the clipping of "Bodo" Reis. I bet he has a cute wife.

It sounds as if winter had come to Madison at last. Here I am again… basking in sunshine while you are all shivering in cold. Uncle Sam sure keeps me away from cold places doesn't he! Maybe I'm speaking too soon! Be careful and don't fall down on the ice.

There sure are a lot of the old gang getting married, all right. Tom, Pep, Phil and I are still holding out though! The fact is, I haven't even got a girl, tsk! Tsk! Oh well, too busy to worry about that today. I still hope Pep and Marge get hitched someday.

The other day we ate K-rations all day. Each meal comes in a small compact box. There is one box for breakfast, one for dinner and one for supper. The food in each differs of course, none is excellent but can be eaten all right. It is really good for a person but doesn't taste too good. I got an extra dinner ration and will send it home the first chance I get. Open it and try it. The food is pure and sealed in. Let me know how you liked it. In the dinner K-ration I will send is a can of Wisconsin cheese which is the best part of the dinner. Will probably be a few days before I send it, however.

My mail is coming in fine now. Sure is wonderful of everyone to write me so often.

Pop, sounds like the poor O.P.A. is having its troubles everyplace doesn't it? Hope you and ration board get straightened out soon.

Another swell day today. Wish you could get in on some of this sunshine. Very nice. Even had some chicken today, bad either. Never could be like you would make it, Mom!

Thanks for the napkin from "Martins," Pop. Time for a class on "guns" again. Bye for today.

Love Bob

·———·

March 13, 1944

Dear folks:

Wow! You should see everyone around here today. We are covered with sand, and I'm not just joking either. We are having a real sand storm today, it has been going on for about seven hours now and still is going strong. Everything is covered with sand, even our blankets on the beds. It is almost impossible to see more than half a block at times. It really stings when it hits us in the face. Sure will be glad when it is over so we can get cleaned up again. I can sure brush plenty of it out of my hair. It isn't raining though, nice and sunny but plenty windy. More fun!!

Today we were reprocessed again as an extra check to be positive our records etc. are all set. Made sure everyone had received all shots, schooling, gunnery range practice, new dog tags, etc. Even took our pictures.

Starting tomorrow we are to take 2 to 2½ hours schooling on malaria, per day for five days. That takes care of a pass for another week. Cannot even get a 24-hour pass while this schooling is going on.

Enclosed you will find a couple of desert flowers which I picked today. There is a little white flower that looks kind of like a lily that I will try to find and send another day.

I think our sand storm will be over in another couple of hours. Outside of being a bit sandy I feel fine. The sand won't hurt us a bit, just gives us a chance to have some time off to shower and wash our hair. I hope you are all as well as I am!

This radar man from Merrill, Wis. and I have a lot of fun together. He seems to be a good kid. He is 21 I believe, and was just married about a month ago. Cute wife too! We have fun going to the show every other night. One theatre, and there is always a line of pairs over two blocks long. This is a fact! This field including landing area is 22 sq. mi. Nice cozy place, eh!

Bye for tonight.

Love Bob

.———.

March 17, 1944

Dear folks:

I got a lot of swell mail today, letters from Kath, Pop, Aunt Maude and Jackie. All were very interesting and swell! Thanks a million to all of you!

I have a box all packed to send to you tomorrow or Monday as the case may be. In it are the following:

One map of the trip from Chicago to Blythe, 4 postcards, one set of views of Utah, one pair of new work gloves for Pop, and one 50 caliber machine gun bullet plus one extra lead slug, also 50 cal. The shells are not dangerous as the powder is dumped out and the cap is exploded. If you don't want the cartridge then please give it to Jack Gay as he collects them. These are the real cartridges fired from the many machine guns on all of our war planes. A mix-up on records, therefore the extra pair of work gloves. Use them, Pop, they are pretty good gloves. The cartridges are in the fingers of the gloves.

Didn't work very hard today. Nice sunny day again, didn't even need a shirt on today.

I hope you are all fine, Yippee too. I feel swell!! Everything is going really fine. Time to hit the sack for a few hours now so good night folks.

Love Bob

.———.

March 19, 1944

Dear folks:

I sure put in a profitable day today. We are getting ready for an extended tour, as I mentioned before. I'll be able to give travel talks on points of interest about the world when I get home to stay.

We had a clothing processing today. They took away all of my summer outfits, caps, trousers, shirts and all. It sure is swell to have all new stuff again, just like the first day in the army. We sure had a lot of fun today.

I think another two or three weeks will see me off to a new destination, probably a P.O.E. someplace.

I have high hopes of getting a pass tomorrow. If I get it Gilbert and I are heading for Mexico. Might be able to get you some silk stockings, we'll see.

I just took a shower and dressed up in new shoes, socks, fatigues, etc. Feel swell!!

I got three very nice white hankies from Jackie for my birthday. Was very nice of her! Got a fine letter from Grandma Gay. Aunt Oly sent me some money for birthday also. Swell of her too!

All for now,

Love Bob

———

El Centro, California
March 20, 1944

Dear Mom:

Gilbert (a pal in the 18th communication dept.) and I got our pass and left camp at 7 p.m. last night. We hitchhiked from Blythe to Indio, to Coachella, past the Salton Sea, Brawley and to El Centro where I am now. We got here at 1 a.m. today, got a room in this hotel and are now up and continuing our trip. We are now only a few miles from the Mexican border, heading for Mexicali, Mexico.

Enclosed in the package are three pair of Mexican nylons, which people here in El Centro tell us are better than the silk; also, there are some little silver gifts.

I want you to have two pairs of hose and Kath to have one pair plus her choice of the gifts for her birthday present from me. I would appreciate it very much if you would send whatever gifts Kath doesn't want to Jackie and Barbara; however, if Kath would like both pin and the bracelet send a pin to Jackie. I think Kath will like the charm bracelet best, but if not give it to Jackie. Just so Kath gets her choice of the gifts and a pair of hose is the main thing. I bought all of them in Mexico this a.m.

I hope everything is O.K. and that you like the hose alright. I hope also that Kath is pleased with her birthday presents O.K. Happy Birthday, Kath!!

Love, Bob

.———.

Blythe, California
34ᵗʰ Bomb Group
18ᵗʰ Bomb Squadron
Army Air Base.
March 23, 1944

Dear Mom, Dad and Kath:

Sorry I didn't get to write yesterday. Have been very busy. Your letters are still coming along in fine shape. I got the box you sent me yesterday. *Thanks* so much. The pictures are swell! I will send the ones I took in Boca Raton home soon. Am going to keep the ones of you because they are so good!! The little cakes were wonderful!! The boys and I thank you from the bottom of our hearts, Mom. *They were sure good!!*

I hope you received the package I sent you from Mexico. We made it back to camp in plenty of time. Had a swell time.

I have been busy stenciling my equipment and clothes lately. We have, besides new clothes, a pup tent, pegs, pole, and today got a neat, strong trench knife and sheath for it. We are to be

Planes were always flying overhead.

issued carbines or submachine gun in a couple of days. I hope I get a machine gun, but probably will get a carbine as only ten per cent of the squadron will get tommy-guns.

Expect to leave here in the *very, very near future*, at least by April 1. May have to send some stuff home eventually as we must get everything into one duffle bag when we leave here. We can carry only 125 pounds of stuff, so I hear.

I hope you can read this letter O.K. as I am writing pretty fast. I sure owe a lot of letters... I hope I can answer each one of them soon.

Time for me to hit the sack for a while, so I'll say good night folks. Take care of yourselves and have fun.

All my love,

Bob

·————·

March 25, 1944

Dear Mom, Dad and Kath:

Please don't worry about it if you don't write each day, Mom. Your letters are so swell and long that I don't see how it is possible to write as often as you do. You're a "peach" Mom!! It was swell to hear about Bob Sasman, Don Oscar, Claude and Jack P. I'm awfully glad Doctor Sullivan's son will be O.K.

I had a really fine time reading all of the papers and magazines that were in the box you sent. The cookies came through perfectly and they were wonderful. The stationery is swell, I can sure use it and the soap. There are two or three of us fellows from Wisconsin who are really enjoying the book. I'm glad you have a fine picture of a B-24. Quite a ship, isn't it. *Thanks* for the Vicks, hankies and socks. I can use all three. Have no cold now, but never can tell!!

Thanks a million for the birthday kiss, Mom dear. It's the only one I got and the one I *wanted most to have*!! You are my best girl, Mom! *You know that!!* You are the only one that is kissing me now, too! Thanks so much for everything!

Enclosed in this letter you will find my driver's license, Social Security card, etc. We have to send home or get rid of everything bearing our home address, squadron or group number before leaving here. Please save the enclosed cards, pictures, etc. for me until I come home. SAVE THEM ALL!!

Things are really interesting now, but I can't tell you much of anything about it. All I can say is that I'll see all I can so I can be a travel expert or something when I get home again.

This is enough for this letter as the enclosures will make it quite heavy. I'm going to write another one to you right after I seal this one.

I'll write "tomorry" or Monday, as the case may be.

Love Bob

.————.

March 28, 1944

Dear Mom, Dad and Kath:

I have had so many fine letters, cards and gifts that my birthday is only lacking one thing. That is being with you! Remember the fun we had at our little party in the Palmer House last year? It sure was fun! Anyway, thanks from the bottom of my heart for all you have done for me!!

Kath—I hope you have a real, wonderful birthday. I know you will. Not only the nice things you will receive will make you happy but also being at home with the best Mom and Dad in the world should make everything complete for you. I hope you have a swell time and are very happy. Thank you very much for the swell letter and birthday card you sent me. They were really swell, honey. Be good and have a real HAPPY BIRTHDAY!!

Don't worry about me because I'm going to be twenty-one tomorrow, you are still my boss and my best girl, Mom!

The girl I met at the P.X. that went to West High with me is Ella Christenson (Swede or Norsky)! She is here with a girl friend who married a soldier here a couple weeks ago. She isn't engaged after all, I guess. Haven't had much chance to talk to her.

Bob in a jeep.

Tomorrow night, Dick Ellis and I are going out to the civilian mess on the field and buy our dinner. They have fine meals there, and we are going to eat out and go to the movie so you see my birthday will not go uncelebrated.

Enclosed is a picture of a B-4, just exactly like the ones I work on.

I finished a roll of film the other day and will mail it in that little bag very soon. No picture of Dick Levenick though. Had to turn in our cameras for shipment.

Pop—thanks for the good articles you send me from your desk. I have a good time reading them. I'm glad things are going so swell about the Monroe St. Apartments, etc.

All for now,

Love Bob

·———·

April 1, 1944

Good morning folks!

Boy! What a beautiful morning it is!! Swell blue sky and plenty of nice warm sunshine. Wish you could be here to enjoy it. Your fine letters have been coming right along. I want to thank you once again for everything. I had a good time on my birthday, even here at Blythe.

I wish I could tell you all about the "goings on" here but I can't say much more than I have said already. We are doing a lot of packing. Yesterday I sent home a box full of clothes. I kept the best underwear, etc. but had to send a lot home as I have absolutely no room for it and we can only take so much. Everything we own must go into one duffle bag, including tent, blankets, etc.

When you receive this letter I believe I'll be far from Blythe, Cal. It will probably be quite a while before you hear from me again as they may hold up our mail after we leave here. So, please don't worry about me. I honestly feel perfect and everything is really fine and dandy.

Oh yes, in that box of clothes I sent home you will find something in the toes of two pair of socks. If you don't want it, I know Jack Gay would be pleased with it.

I have plenty of money as we were paid last night, and I also did O.K. for my birthday. Everyone remembered me, it seems.

I haven't been in Arizona but at least I can see it from my barracks. We are only seven miles from the line. Can see some mountains from here that are in Arizona. All the mountains near here are barren, desolate ones.

Bye for now,
Love Bob

May 24, 1945

Dear Bobbins,

So glad to hear from you today — the first since V.E. Even so it still hasn't improved the mail service any - 15 days yet.

Naturally the nicest news was your "hunch" about coming home. Knowing you, that must be pretty definite. You never did say things you didn't mean. I'm keeping my fingers very tightly crossed for you, now. I told the kids & they practically jumped for joy. Philly Stark is coming home next month & Dick Burke will be in Madison this weekend. Honest to god, it seems so funny really talking about it & knowing for sure it's actually happening. Everybody's been

dreaming about it for so long, comprenez-vous?

Well be prepared for a shock, brother. Margi received a diamond from the Tracy man this week. It will be in the paper Sunday. I can, I believe it after about a six weeks acquaintance but it's none of my business. At just doesn't sound Margi. I can't help but wonder how Kay is taking it all. The boy is very nice & from a very good family from Long Island. He's about 6 ft with average looks but it still seems funny.

The doctor's vacationing so Jackie's playing, to a certain extent. It's kind of fun being completely in charge. I've just learned to give x-ray therapy treatments. I'm still a little scared 'cause if I didn't do everything just

super x-ray burn & he said it won't. Now don't you worry, I'll be good & conscientious & very careful, I promise!

The weather I hope has finally taken a turn for the better, but every weekend it rains so I keep crossing like mad (under my breath of course). Everybody's playing since school's out — to be truthful I'm a little jealous when they talk about canoeing & fooling around. Guess it must be my lazy nature. Coming out spring fever's a little late this year I guess.

Eddie Samp is coming through pretty well but I guess he really got a lot of shrapnel in his head.

Did you know Mr. Spell died of pneumonia Monday? He was only sick ten days. We all feel so bad about it. It's going to

be tough on the boys to get such awful news so far away from everybody & everything close to them. Richard's been over for about 2 yrs. now too.

Well son, it's terrifically late so must close for now. All I can say now is hurry home, I hope!!

as ever,
Jackie

CHAPTER 11

CAMP MYLES STANDISH, MASSACHUSETTS

April 8, 1944

Dear Mom, Dad and Kath:

Here is the long-lost son again. I'm sure jumping around in a hurry, aren't I? I'm in the eastern part of the United States and I feel fine.

I caught a slight cold coming here but I feel much better today. The food here is pretty good and it is a pleasure to eat off trays again. I can only tell you some of the states I came through on my way here. [The states were cut out by the censor.] You can see that I've added a few more states to my travels.

The weather here isn't too cold but it is rainy and unpleasant at this time.

I'm with a good bunch of fellows and we have quite a bit of fun together.

This letter probably won't be very interesting but it is hard to write under a mess of rules. I'll get on to it better before long, I hope.

I hope Easter Day is a nice day and that you have a nice time. Please say "Hello" to everyone.

Take care of yourselves and have fun.

Bye for now—

Love, Bob

NOTE FROM MOM

Bob phoned from the East Coast on the 9th.

AUTHOR'S NOTE

There would be no letters sent home during the next few weeks as Bob was prepped and transported to Liverpool. It would be just over a year before Bob could share any of that journey with his family, like the nine-day journey over the ocean on a converted transport, the zig-zag pattern they took, what direction they went, etc. It was made clear that it could endanger the guys who would travel after them: "Loose lips sink ships."

CHAPTER 12

MENDLESHAM, ENGLAND

May 3, 1944

Dear Mom, Dad, and Kath,

There are many things that I cannot write to you at the present time, including my location, but I hope to be able to tell you more in the near future.

Mom, I hope you are over your cold by the time this letter gets on the way.

I'm sure glad I called home when I did. It was wonderful to hear each of you.

I sure do approve of your buying Kath a horse. It was really swell of you to do it, Pop. I guess she has proven that she really wanted one. She will really have a wonderful time with it. Maybe, if she will get it tame enough by the time I get home again I'll be able to take a little ride, O.K.?

I'm awfully glad you had such a wonderful birthday party, Pop. I'd have given an awful lot to have been there. I'm sorry I didn't get you a present but it was kind of impossible to do so at that time.

Gosh, I guess all the old gang will be married by the time I get home again. Well, I'm glad there will still be plenty of beautiful American girls left to choose from when I get back. Haven't much time to worry about it now anyhow.

Enough for tonite. Take good care of yourselves and have fun.
Good night,
Bob.

May 11, 1944

Dear Mom, Dad and Kath:

Our old Uncle Sam sure does take your son on some quaint trips, doesn't he! Here I am in Jolly Old England, feeling fine and raring to go! It is really very interesting to see the new customs and so forth. That is, they are new to us. I'm doing pretty well learning the British money system. I'll send some money home for souveniers [*sic*] after a time.

I'm even getting used to driving on the opposite side of the road. It sure seems funny though. The countryside is very nice. The fields and farms are the neatest kept of any I have ever seen. Most all of the fields are divided by pretty green hedges and often by flowers, also. It seems as if every square inch of land is being used to produce food. The English people are really working hard. They keep their horses in the best condition I have ever seen. Their coats are fine and shiny and really are beautiful to see. The work horses are huge animals with heavy manes, large hair-covered feet, and bushy tails.

It seems as if everyone here rides a bike. Old and young alike can always be seen peddling along the roads.

I have had a few short passes so far, but have managed to see a few towns and cities. They are very interesting but far different from anything at home. Someday I'll be able to tell you about a lot of interesting things I've seen. Most everything is built of brick and cement.

Pop, you should see some of these British Fords. They are very small, as are most cars here. They don't even look like a Ford.

Mom, I sent you a Mother's Day cablegram. I hope you got it O.K. Sorry I can't get a nice big bouquet of flowers for you. You are the best mom in the world!

The weather has been pretty fair so far and we are taking advantage of it by a bit of walking around. As you said, Pop, "See everything you can while you have the chance." Well, I'm sure doing it.

Our living conditions are pretty fair, in that they are better than some camps in the U.S., so please don't worry about me as everything is fine.

We changed our American money for English money just after we arrived. I'm making out plenty O.K. In fact I'll probably be able to save a bit of money for a change.

The English people are very polite and very busy. They really know what war is like. When I think how we all complained about a very few inconveniences at home, I'm actually ashamed. People in the States don't have a complaint in the world. They live in luxury compared to the English.

We have a P.X. here and get a certain ration each week. It's really pretty good at that. We get two bars of candy, one package of gum, one bar of soap, two razor blades, one small package of plain cookies, seven packages of cigarettes or four packages of pipe tobacco. We get all this once a week for the equivalent of about 82 cents. Not bad, eh? I usually give away the smokes to the boys or else trade them for a bar of candy or something.

We sure would love to get a box of candy, cookies, cheese and crackers every now and then. I guess we have to request things in order to have anything sent to us, so I'll probably request fairly often. Please don't try to send something every time I ask for it, but by doing that you'll always have my request if you happen to have something on hand so it can be sent. O.K? I hope so. Take good care of yourselves and say "Hello" to everyone.

All my love,
Bob

·————·

May 19, 1944

Dear Mom, Pop and Kath:

Yes, Mom, I get K.P. once in a while, too. I just finished one week of it yesterday. Everyone below the grade of tech. sergeant must do K.P. for one week every so often. I won't get it again for quite a few weeks now. Outside of that week I have been working hard applying my education. Keeping plenty busy, too!

By now you must know that I'm in England. I'm sending this letter by Air-Mail. I wish you would tell me if Air-Mail makes better time than V-Mail. Your Air-Mail letters usually beat the

V-Mail by two to three days. When you do write V-Mail it is by far easier to read when typewritten. I don't have any trouble reading handwritten V-Mail of yours but some people write too small. I know I have at times.

We have now got a radio in our mission hut. We get a lot of swell programs which some does more than you can imagine to keep us all happy. We get swell American programs especially broadcast for the American troops in the European Theater of Operations. Bob Hope, Bing Crosby, Mickey Rooney, Judy Garland, etc.

We can listen to a lot of foreign countries' broadcasts over the radio in our hut. We sure get a laugh out of the broadcasts from Germany. We can listen to them almost any evening or late afternoon. In fact we hear the best dance music over the German stations. Most of the good dance music is American. They spend hours every day broadcasting in English to our invasion forces. They play a lot of our dance music because they know it will attract our attention. They play good music for ten minutes then talk propaganda for a while, then music again. We really get a lot of fun listening to them. We hear Lord Haw Haw, an English traitor whom you have probably read about, give his daily broadcast. If you think the German claims you read and hear about at home are queer, you should hear directly from them as we do. They sure must take us for dopes! I'll have some good stories to tell you when I get home again. We also hear many other foreign broadcasts but I can't understand them.

Our huts in which we live are not half bad. They are fairly comfortable and we have a lot of fun living in them. There are seventeen of us in my barracks. Really a good bunch of boys on the whole. Have some good times together. So you see folks, we always manage to have fun regardless of where we are.

Will write again tomorrow or next day.

All my love,

Bob.

•———•

Bob by a B-24 "Liberator" in England.

May 23, 1944

Dear folks:

Here is the letter I promised to write yesterday. Sorry I couldn't write as I promised, but as we are kept very busy I just didn't get a chance.

We work at any hour day or night. Really would make a good income at $1.00 an hour for every hour we work. There just isn't any eight- or ten-hour shifts over here. We are always on the job, but at the same time we somehow manage to get some time for a bit of fun. There is a different movie here almost every night. We don't have a nice theatre with comfortable seats like the ones in the States. It is just another building, a bit larger than the others with rows of wooden benches and a sound system that would scare the people at home.

Over here, however, it is plenty O.K. and we sure do enjoy seeing a show once in a while. We also got double rations so far as candy is concerned. Really was good, too! Made us all pretty happy. We do get a chance to have fun regardless of how many hours we work. Have plenty of laughs in the hut and on the line.

Mom, I'm glad you enjoy working at the U.S.O., etc. Really got a good laugh from the clipping about the "Grocery Girl."

Keep feeling good and don't catch any colds. I'm fine and all is O.K.

All for now,

Love Bob

Kath sure is doing O.K. in school. Nice going, kid! Have fun and give your horse a chunk of sugar for me.

•———•

May 27, 1944

Dear Mom, Pop, and Kath,

Hi everyone! I hope you all are fine. I feel very good and I sure don't have any trouble finding enough to keep me busy! There is plenty of work for me every day.

Bob feeling swell.

We just heard another program from Germany on the radio. To tell you the truth we really get a lot of enjoyment out of them. I don't see how they expect us to believe their stories but they do play good American music. I must admit that they are very clever even though they often seem foolish.

Well folks, I'm fine and everything is swell and hope that you are also fine.

[Cut out by the censor.]

All my love, Bob

·————·

June 3, 1944

Dear Mom, Dad and Kath:

This was a very lucky day for me because I received ten fine letters ranging from May 16 to the 25.

Dad, you asked whether the bomber group or the squadron should come first in my address, so as far as I know the squadron should be first. Either way will be O.K. however.

I'm glad you are keeping newspaper articles for the scrapbook, particularly the one that Capt. Brechler wrote. It should be exceptionally good!

I'll bet Yippee really looks swell!

Ellis and I live in the same hut, Mom. Kelly, Fernandes and Glenn are in different sections of the camp but I see them quite often. They belong to other squadrons. There are 17 of us living in our Nissen hut, a pretty good gang for the most part.

Please return a "Hello" to Mrs. Prideaux and tell her that I haven't started dropping my *h*'s as yet. You must be having quite a good time with the drill team, U.S.O., etc. I'm glad you are, Mom.

Yes, Mom, I still wear my flannel shirts, we don't have khakis here. I hope Kath had a good time at Neal's. I imagine she did, especially since he has some riding horses.

Pop, thanks for your congratulations on my stripe but it really is nothing to celebrate as I should have been way past there a long time ago. Guess I just hit a few bad breaks along that line but I'm not worrying about it cause it would do me very little good.

THANK YOU BOTH FOR YOUR EXTRA SWELL LETTERS. THEY MEAN AN AWFUL LOT TO ME.

All my love,

Bob.

·————·

June 9, 1944

Dear Mom, Dad and Kath:

The mailman has been extremely good to me the last two days. Nothing is as good to see as a neat letter or so when we return to our hut each day. All of the letters were wonderful and all I can say is: thank you all very much for writing!

Mom, you asked me how I received my mail. Well, sometimes I don't get any for three or four days and then get a nice stack, then again sometimes it comes each day. Very uneven. They all get here sooner or later and that is what counts. Mom, I'm glad your garden is coming so fine. I think both you and Dad are enjoying it a lot.

You asked who was my seamstress, Mom. Well, I've no sewing to be done so I just don't have any seamstress. If there is any sewing to be done I guess I'll have to do it myself. I'll be a good all-around kid when I get out of this army. I can wash, cook, sew, and eat a lot of foods I'd never touched before. When you are really hungry you can eat most anything they will dish out. We get plenty to eat here. It is pretty sad stuff a great deal of the time, but we get a pretty fair army meal every now and then. We get a lot more butter than I ever expected to see in England.

Say, Pop, thanks for the addresses. I'll be sure to use them. How was the Decoration Day parade? Or did it get rained out? Glad Kath had such a fine time on her little trip.

This is evidently letter writing night in our hut. Most of the fellows are doing just as I am, just sitting on the bed writing for all they are worth. I know you must wonder why I don't write you more about what's what, but I know you can understand why. Lots to tell you some day. I still haven't had a chance to get any snapshots, but I'll get them one of these days, if the sun will only stay out long enough.

Thanks again for all the good letters and the stationery.

Have fun,

Love Bob

·———·

June 18, 1944

Dear Dad:

Today is Father's Day and I hope it is an extra swell one for you. I'm awfully sorry I couldn't send you a nice gift but want you to know that I didn't forget about it. I'm thinking of you, Pop. You're the best there is!

Love, Bob

Dear Mom, Dad and Kath:

Hello folks, how's everyone today? I hope you are all feeling fine. It is a swell day today for a change, sunny and fairly warm.

Well, I bought me a pretty nice English bicycle a few days ago. In fact a few of us bought bikes on the same day. Our barracks now has six bicycles sitting alongside. They cost us a pretty penny but I've already had more fun and seen more of England than I have since I've been here. I'm really glad I got it because I have had a really swell time so far. It is rapidly paying for itself. I've had two nice trips on it so far. The first one was approximately 30 miles and the second one was approximately 58 mi. Yesterday Jack Campbell, of Oakland, California, and I had the afternoon off. We left Camp around 1:00 p.m. and just started riding. We visited four villages and one fairly large city. It was a very interesting trip and we certainly did enjoy getting out for a swell ride through the country. Everything is green and very nice to see. I'll no doubt see a lot more of this country on my bike than any other way. We just had the best time we have had since we've been here. I'm keeping a record of where I've been so someday we can add it to our book, Mom. We rode from 1:00 p.m. until midnight. Really slept awfully well last night!

Oh boy! I just got my mail and what a swell day this is! I got the package with the clothes, Mom. that picture of Kath on the horse's wonderful!! I just can't tell you how swell it is. Kath, you and the horse are both beautiful! I'm crazy about that picture. I'm going to put it up on the wall where I can see it every minute I am in the hut. Gee, thanks from the very bottom of my heart! You sure are a pretty girl, Kath! All the boys are nuts to know you. Just can't blame them after a picture like that! Thanks again! My morale is up 100%!

Yes folks, D-Day was quite a day. We are just as glad to see it underway over here as the people at home are.

Pop, it sounds as you and Mom are having a busy time of it. Mom, with the U.S.O., Red Cross, etc. and you with the lawn, furnace, and ration board. I'm glad both of you are having fun, though. Keep it up! I bet it was funny when you broke the water pipe and got a squirt in the face.

Say, Kath, I'd sure like to see your new boyfriend. He sounds like a swell guy. I hope I get to see him before he withers away from your cooking. Tsk! Tsk! Don't forget your big brother wants to be home to see you get married. Besides, I want to stand by the cutie that catches the flowers. O.K.? I sure hope so! Anyway, whenever you do decide to get married I want to see that everything is done up right. Don't forget about all the guys over here that want to see you. Maybe I'll be home when school is out next year. I hope so!

All for now.

All my love,

Bob.

•———•

June 22, 1944

Dear Mom, Dad and Kath:

We had another nice day today. That makes two in a row. Really quite an event for England. Well, I really feel swell and I sure hope each of you feel just as good.

Instead of using the G.I. laundry service here, I take my stuff over to an English farm near here and the lady of the house does a fair job for me. We can only send nine pieces per week to the G.I. laundry but I can send all I want to this lady. The farm folks around here seem very glad to get laundry from us as it gives them a chance to pick up a little extra money. They certainly charge us very little for the amount of work they do. No one seems to be able to press clothes very well over here. I'm certainly not complaining about that though. We are getting along swell especially in comparison to what it could be like.

Bob and his English bike.

Our camp is located in a very pretty spot. In fact right now from the hut door I can sit here on the bed and look over some very pretty green fields and trees. When you eventually do get some snapshots from me you will see some of the views I can see from my hut. I took a bunch of pictures of the boys while we were cleaning out the hut yesterday. We had beds, blankets, etc. all outside. Also are a few shots of my good friend Jack Campbell and I on our bikes. I hope they turn out well.

I feel swell, am getting along just fine, and get plenty to eat. We get more butter here than we got at any camp except good old Truax. Milk just isn't to be had but we have plenty of coffee, tea and water to drink. You can easily see that we are doing all right. However, I'm dreaming of the day when I can be home with the three of you and have some of those wonderful meals of Mom's.

Well I guess I've rambled on for long enough so I sign off for today. Keep well and have fun.

Love, Bob

P.S. Enclosed is a 10-shilling note which is worth two dollars and two cents today. Please let me know if you got it so I can send a different denomination. Hold it to light and notice ladies' picture in center bottom of note.

· ——— ·

June 28, 1944

Dear folks:

I'm glad to hear that you are well and having fun. Mom, I got your letter of June 18 today. It was a wonderful letter Mother. Thank you very much! I really enjoyed hearing all the news.

Don't feel too sorry for the guys at Truax, Mom. They are darn lucky to have a day off, get laundry done in only two weeks, and a million other things. I have been very fortunate with my laundry, etc., but others here have it a lot tougher.

Mom, thanks for your swell offer to send packages to all the boys in the hut but everyone is getting packages pretty regularly now so I guess it won't be necessary. It was awfully sweet of you to think of it though, Mom.

Pop, I'm glad to hear that the old Olympic has put out the catsup bottles again. The war must be just about over, eh? I can't place the girl you mentioned, Mom. Don't remember anyone by that name of Barigan. Mom, did you get all the candles lit at the O.E.S. party O.K.? Yes, Mom, I get a letter from most all the boys every now and then.

A small part of the collected money Bob sent home.

We listen to a German program most every night. There is a girl named "Midge" on the best program. She was born in America, I believe. She plays good American dance numbers and then gives a little talk between each record. She asks us what our girls and wives are doing, where we think they are, etc. She tries to tell us that we are fighting the war for the English and asks why the Americans haven't learned a lesson from the last war that it doesn't pay to meddle with European affairs, etc. Tells us anything to make us think we are losing the war. All a lot of bunk! But as I said, the music is swell!!

All is well with me.

Love Bob

Enclosed is a three pence piece which is worth 5 cents in our money.

.————.

June 30, 1944

Dear Mom, Dad and Kath:

How's everyone today? I hope you are all fine and dandy, and enjoying better weather than you had a while back.

I really got a great laugh out of a letter I got from Pepper and Marge today. They were out on a date at the French Village and they decided to write me a letter. All they could find to write on were two receipts, of Marge's, from the Madison Musicians Association. Each is the size of a dollar bill. It was a swell letter and awfully good of them to write me. Good old Pep and Marge! What a pair they are!

Of today's news I have three things that are of interest. First, we were awarded the Presidential Citation. It is a blue ribbon with a gold frame around it, which is the only ribbon that can be worn on the right breast. Secondly, we were paid, and last of all I got a hair-cut! Quite a day in the old E.T.O. (European Theater of Operations).

Well, I guess that's about all for today, folks. Keep well, keep happy, and have fun!

All my love,

Bob.

P.S. Enclosed is a sixpence which is worth ten cents in American money.

·———·

July 2, 1944

Dear Mom, Dad and Kath:

Today has been an exceptionally warm, sunny, and cheerful day for us. We just came back from a good U.S.O. show. Had a lot of fun at the show.

The Red Cross has fixed up a very nice recreation building for us. There is a small library, a large reading room, and a snack bar where we can get a couple of sandwiches, coffee or a Coke each night from 7:30 to 10:30. It really is pretty nice. Those Cokes sure taste good!

On Sunday the country roads are full of people both old and young: babies, girls, boys, mothers, fathers, and grandparents. They are either on bicycles or just walking along enjoying themselves. Really seems quite strange in comparison to home.

We can go to a fairly large city not so far away and go to a show, walk around, look over the stores, walk about the park, and eat at the Red Cross. It is interesting to see once or twice but then the novelty wears off. Oh yes, there are plenty of pubs (taverns) around for the boys to drink ale, bitters, etc., but that doesn't bother me any. There are good American movies but they are quite old and we have seen most of them. Besides, we can go to a movie here most every night if we aren't working. There are quite a few girls around, but I've not seen any that exactly knock me out. I'll stick to the wonderful American girl. The best in the world! In fact, anything American is the best in the world! That, all of us agree on.

Well folks, I guess that's all for today. I'm fine, in good spirits, and hope the same is true for each of you. Keep well, keep happy and have fun.

All my love, Bob.

Enclosed is a half crown, which is worth 2 & 6, or two shillings and six pence. (Fifty cents in American money.) How would you like to carry a stack of pound notes in your wallet, Pop? Quite large notes, eh?

•———•

July 5, 1944

Dear Mom, Dad and Kath:

Hello folks, glad to know you are feeling fine and having fun. How do you like my "snappy" stationery which I just got at the P.X.? Maybe I can keep the lines straight for a change. We'll see!

Kath, thanks a lot for the swell letter. It was good to hear from you again and to know that you are really having such a dandy summer. As for a name for your colt, I think you can pick a far better one than I. I like Gay-Way, Moonshine, Sad Sack (no reflection meant on your colt), Snappy, Tops, or maybe Hot Foot? Pretty sad flock of names but just thought I'd send them along.

Yesterday, I went to a city near here and spent a very enjoyable day. I met a very nice girl with blond hair and blue eyes. She has a "Yank" boy-friend but I did enjoy talking with her. I found out quite a bit about England, the people, etc. She had a date with her boy-friend at five o'clock, but I'm afraid she was a half hour late as my watch was wrong. Tsk! Tsk! Hope the boy-friend wasn't too mad at her as they had been going together for over six months. Still say there are no girls like the American girls! I'll have to get busy and find one when I get home.

Folks, I hope you had a fine 4th of July. Plenty of fireworks for Hitler's boys was the main attraction over here.

Enclosed are an English penny, worth two cents U.S. money, and a half penny, worth one cent U.S. money.

All for now, love

Bob

·———·

July 6, 1944

[This was the first air mail letter that showed Bob's new title: corporal.]

Dear folks:

Today has been very fine in two ways. The weather is swell and the old mail boat must have come in. I got seven wonderful letters and the V-Mail newspaper of June 19.

Mom, your dreams are pretty good, aren't they. I kinda thought Jack was going to be married when you wrote. Jack is quite the boy I guess. I hope he has a swell wife. Will be glad to hear more about him when you have talked to his mother.

I'm glad Dick's folks are able to give you some dope on what's what. Ought to be pretty good information.

I'm sure Kath had a fine time at Milwaukee. She and Neal are really enjoying the summer, aren't they! I'm glad she is having so much fun. Don't forget to tell me about the Madison Riding Club's show.

The Red Cross Club here is called the "Aero" Club and really is quite pleasant. I'm sitting at a desk in the club writing this letter, in fact. Pretty nifty having a club, don't you think?

I've got a flat tire on my bike so I'll have to go to work on it one of these days. Just like high school days except I can't send it to the Tursky Cycle Shop to be fixed. Here I do all my work at the Gay-Campbell bicycle shop.

We now have music in the mess hall while we eat, too. It is played on a phonograph from the Special Service Office. Pretty soft! I must admit!

Well folks, one of the boys just reminded me that it is time for chow, so I'll have to go and get the steaks while they are still hot! Oh boy! What a life!

All kidding aside folks, I'm fine, feel swell, and hoping you are even better.

All for now, love

Bob

·———·

Gay Advanced

Robert L. Gay, an Eighth air force radio mechanic for B-24 Liberators based in England, has been promoted to corporal. The son of Mr. and Mrs. Len R. Gay, 702 Baltzell st., Corp. Gay is a graduate of West high school and attended the university. His division has been cited for the historic England-Africa shuttle bombing of Messerschmitt aircraft plants at Regensburg, Germany in August, 1943.

Capital Times
9-18-44

Gay Promoted

EIGHTH AIR FORCE BOMBER STATION, England— Robert L. Gay, 21, son of Mr. and Mrs. Len R. Gay, 702 Baltzell st., has been promoted to a corporal at his Liberator bomber station.

A radio mechanic, Corp. Gay is a graduate of West high school and was a student at the University of Wisconsin before entering the army air force.

He is a member of the Third bombardment division, cited by the president for its now historic England-Africa shuttle bombing of the Messerschmitt aircraft plants at Regensburg, Germany, in August, 1943. Corp Gay helps maintain the radio equipment installed in the B-24 bombers.

Capital Times and *Wisconsin State Journal* articles about Bob's promotion.

July 8, 1944

Dear Mom, Dad and Kath:

Say, Dad, that fancy stationery is plenty O.K.

We all got a big kick out of that! That sounds like quite a hotel, on quite a well-known beach! You sure can pick 'em, Pop. Thanks a lot for writing.

Shall I buy a jeep after the war? I see that the servicemen overseas will have first chance at them for "only" $500.00. They would be alright to go on picnics or fishing but outside of that they wouldn't be so hot. In my opinion they wouldn't be worth $100.00, and even then I'd rather put it towards a red Ford or something.

Am getting plenty to eat, feel fine, and can't complain about a thing.

Have fun and keep well, love

Bob

July 10, 1944

Dear Mom, Dad and Kath:

I get the *Stars and Stripes* which is the Army's official news-paper every day except Sunday so am able to keep up with the news pretty well. Of course the radio helps a good deal, also. I'm glad that Dewey made out so well in Chicago. I'm sure glad Lee Haskin made West Point. He is a swell guy and I know he will do plenty O.K.

Well, the reason I didn't mention the price of my bike was because I thought you might think it unreasonable. To tell you the truth, it was unreasonable but there was little choice if I wanted a bike. I paid 14 pounds or $56.00 in our money. It is a light weight, very narrow-tired bike and it cannot compare in any way to an American bicycle, but it does the trick alright! My bike at home is much stronger and rides a lot better. This bike peddles very easily as it is so light. I'm glad you are pleased that I bought it. I really am having a lot of fun on it so I believe it is paying for itself. It is in very good shape as it was only three weeks old when I bought it. Our hut now has seven bicycles. We are really a well to do gang of "rough riders." The bikes at this hut cost from 7 to 17 pounds each. Most were 13, 14 or 15 pounds. A pound is equal to $4.00. Mom, you said you hoped I had enough money with me when I got the bike. I did, Mom, and had some left over, in fact.

Not an awful lot to write about as to what I've been doing lately, but I do hope to get in some more bike trips in the near future. I am keeping a little map of all the places I've been going to, so someday I'll be able to show you. I have been to seven towns and one large city on my bike, plus many other places that I saw on the way to this field.

Dad, if the soldiers keep the same ideas after the war as they have now I believe Gay Brothers will be able to do quite a bit of building. Small, attractive homes seem to be on a lot of minds. Hope they are still there after the war.

I'm really learning a lot of interesting things about most everything. It sure would amaze the average person to know the work, cost, and time it takes to "keep 'em flying" as they say.

I sure do miss all of you! All is O.K. here and I'm starting to drowse off so better say good-night.

Really am getting along quite fine with our rations, etc. Mom, but can always use some candy and cookies. They're awfully good!

All my love,

Bob

·———·

July 12, 1944

Dear Mom, Dad and Kath:

I hope all of you are feeling swell and enjoying a wonderful summer. I feel swell but I miss all of you very much. It will be the happiest day of my life when I get home and see my mom, dad and sister again.

Things here are running along about as usual. We are keeping up a pretty good pace and I'm sure old Uncle Adolph would be very happy if we were to leave here. Everything is O.K. and I'm fine. I must say that I can really sleep when I finally do hit the sack.

We do about the same thing every day, get up, work, eat, work, eat, work, eat, see a show or get off a few letters, Someday I'll be able to tell you all but it's time to hit the sack again. The happenings and other things that are always going on here.

How is my dog behaving this summer? I'll bet she is having a wonderful time.

You know, when I get home I think I'll just take a couple of weeks off and just take life easy. It will be wonderful to sleep in my good old bed again. Almost have forgotten how it feels to live such a wonderful life. Well, that will make it even better when I do get home.

Well, I guess you can see that I've been doing a lot of day-dreaming about you, home, and so on—but it really is fun to think about it.

Take good care of yourselves and have lots of fun.

All my love,

Bob

July 17, 1944

Dear Mom, Dad and Kath:

Hi folks, I'm awfully sorry I haven't written for a few days but I've been plenty busy for the past week and have had little time.

Before I get started I want to congratulate you, Kath. I think it's wonderful that you have a ring. Neal must be a real guy to get such a peach of a girl! I hope, with all my heart that I'll be home to attend the big event when it takes place. Please do send me a picture of Neal as I'd like to see him. He must be quite the boy!

To say that I was surprised to hear that you are engaged would be an understatement. It just doesn't seem possible that my little sister has grown up so fast. Well, honey, I'm sure pitching for you, and I'm awfully happy too!

Mom, in your letter of July 1 you said that you dreamed that I made corporal. Your dream was pretty good as you well know by now. I made corporal just two days after your dream, Mom. I made it on July 1.

You know, Mom, if it weren't for your letters I don't see how I would know what the date was around here. Whenever anyone starts writing in here they always have to ask the date, day and often the month. Time makes little difference to us as we keep busy and will do the same tomorrow as we have done today.

It will be quite some time before I can get any snapshots to you. Up to July 15. All films had to be sent to London to be developed and censored. It took approx. 2 to 3 months to get them back, but now we hand them in to the P.X. so I think we will get better service.

The farm folks, and most everyone else are very polite to us and seem happy that the Yanks are fighting with the English. However, the people here are not very fond of the Yanks and the Yanks are not especially fond of the English either. I know that, with very few exceptions, I'm not especially nuts about them. Well, nevertheless we all get along with each other pretty well just the same.

Bob behind his Nissen hut on his base in England. On the back, he wrote: "Some pose, eh!"

You mentioned seeing a beautiful plane go over the house the other day. Yes, I'm working on the same kind, Mom. They are really pretty in the sky aren't they!

Pop, you might give Chuck Topp my congratulations on his new son. Thanks a lot!

Well folks, I guess I'll end this letter as it is getting quite long and it's time to hit the sack. I'm glad you are all feeling so well, and having such good times.

I'm fine and everything is okey doke. I'll write again tomorrow, I promise. Take good care of yourselves and have fun.

Good night,

Love, Bob

Bob showing off his jacket beside his Nissen hut in England.

———

July 18, 1944

Dear Mom, Dad and Kath:

Hi folks, here is my today's communique from the European Theater of Operations.

The weather today is as usual, which means that it is plenty sad. We are averaging about one and one-half nice days per week now. Quite a lot of cloudy weather in this region of the world.

We are listening to the nightly German news broadcasts at the present. They can really twist their defeats around so they appear like German victories. They are still plenty cocky, but do not brag about themselves like they did when we first arrived.

You asked about the robot bombs, Mom. None have come over our field, but some have hit just a very few miles away. Over here the pilotless plane's favorite name is the "Buzz Bomb." They are certainly no joke and can do plenty of damage. However, the "Jerries" will, and are paying dearly for each Buzz Bomb they send over. Please don't worry about me as I'm fine and everything is okey doke as I've told you before.

I just heard a cute little poem over the radio that goes as follows: Roses are red, violets are blue; I know Violet's are blue because I saw them hanging on the line yesterday. O.K! O.K! I know—but I did hear it over the radio, honest!

The roofs over here are very interesting, especially on the farm houses as they are made of straw. Huge thatched roofs that really must do the trick all right. I'll try to get a snap-shot of one to send home.

Dad, so far as I know, all of the boys are receiving packages, etc. from their homes quite regularly. However, if I do find someone who isn't as fortunate as the rest of us I'll be sure to let you know. It sure was swell of you to offer to help some of the boys out, Dad.

All for now, folks. Good night, all my love

Bob

———

July 20, 1944

Dear Mom, Dad and Kath:

I've sent two or three copies of the *Stars and Stripes* to you by regular mail. I hope you enjoy reading them as they are our best news source outside of the radio, and we really like 'em!

It's quite interesting to listen to the English news broadcasts and then switch directly to the German broadcasts. Sometimes they agree, sometimes show indifference, and other times they disagree. Wish you folks could listen to them as we do. More fun!

Mom, I got your fine letters of July 7 and 8. Thanks a million. Mom, you asked about the Presidential Citation we received. The whole 34th Bomb Group got it. The citation is given for "outstanding performance of duty in action." The Bomb Group consists of a few squadrons.

You also asked if I wanted some more clothes sent to me. I guess I could probably use what socks are good but I have plenty of others to last for quite a while. So if you want to send the socks I'll wear them out alright, Mom. Eh yes, please send the handkerchiefs along, too.

We have quite a few different trees over here. Quite a few choke-cherry trees, some elms (not American elms though), chestnut, and oaks. As far as flowers are concerned I haven't paid too much attention, but have noticed a lot of tulips, ragged robins, violets, poppies, snow drops and bachelor buttons. I'm not much of a florist but between the boys and myself we figured out a few of them. How did we do?? There are an awful lot of wild poppies growing all over the place. I'll try to press one and send it to you.

We aren't bothered much by mosquitoes but we do have a million and one other little bugs that pester us quite a bit, especially on the warmer days.

It was good to hear about Melvin and Red. We know we are lucky to live in huts instead of tents. It gets pretty cool during the night here and we would feel it plenty if we lived in a tent.

We haven't had much of anything exciting to write about for a few days now. A buzz bomb came over the field a couple of nights ago but didn't hit us here. We have had very little trouble with the flying bombs so far and even though they may go over us now and then there is nothing to worry about. After all we are a very small target for such an inaccurate weapon. When a buzzer goes over we just hope it has enough gas in it to keep on going.

Please don't worry about me as everything is fine. I feel very good and can put away my share of the chow.

I saw a good movie tonight. Sure made me wish I was doing a bit of dating with a cute little blonde or brunette.

Good night, folks. All my love,

Bob

.———.

July 25, 1944

Dear Mom, Dad and Kath:

Gee, here I am way behind in my letters again. Sorry, I'll try to catch up right now.

Folks, your letters are swell! They have all the news I like to hear about in them. Only wish my letters to you could be as interesting.

My bike is still in pretty good shape and very popular with all the boys both in and out of our hut. I've had one flat so far. Not bad at that considering the quality of the tires. Bob Ames is certainly getting along quite well, isn't he! He must be in fine health again. I'm sure glad he got in the Navy O.K.

You can add New Mexico, Texas and Arizona to our list, Mom.

You mentioned Sgt. Grimm in your letter of July 11, Mom. The last letter I got from him was written on April 21, I believe.

Say Mom, how old is Neal's sister Helen, and what does she look like? Tsk! Tsk!!

I'm glad that Jack Prideaux and his wife got home for a few days. I'll bet he was a proud boy to get home and show his new wife to the folks, etc. All I can do is wish him the best of luck and hope that he doesn't get shipped out now.

Dad, I am happy to know that we are getting a new roof on the house. What color are the shingles? You and Mom must keep awfully busy between the office, garden and ration board. Kath being busy with her fiance and horse, and I over here makes us quite a busy family, doesn't it!

Time for me to hit the good old sack for a few hours so I'll say good night, and have fun.

All my love, Bob

P.S. Thanks again for all the swell letters from each of you. Keep well and give my best to everyone. I'll write again tomorrow.

Love, Bob

•————•

July 30, 1944

Dear Mom, Dad and Kath:

Boy! We have had four days of absolutely fine weather now. Must be sort of a record here to have that number of nice days in succession.

I'm really very sorry I've been so slow in writing the last few weeks. It seems as if each time I would start to write, something would come up to make me put it off for a while.

Starting the day after tomorrow, August 1 we can turn in our exposed films to be developed. So eventually some pictures will get home. I hope they turn out O.K.

Kath, I'm very glad to hear that you are so happy. I can easily understand why! You're a peach, Kath! That man of yours must be a real guy. I only wish I could actually meet him. After this war is over I'll get my wish won't I? I know I will!! I'm anxious to hear from you again, Kath. Please write soon.

The crops over here look O.K. I guess. Our hut is bounded on two sides with oats and wheat. They both must be about ready to cut.

Mom, I've got plenty of tire patches and as new bicycle tires are easy to obtain I think I'll make out O.K.

I'm glad I sent that English money home when I did as we can no longer send coins in the mail.

I feel mighty good and hope you are feeling even better than I!

Keep well, keep happy, and have fun!

Your loving son,

Bob.

P.S. Always like to receive a nice box of candy. One of the boys got a box of Whitman's Samplers today and it came through in fine shape.

.————.

August 3, 1944

Dear Kath:

Hello Sis! How was that trip to Lake Delevan with the Alpha Gamma girls? I'll bet you really had a swell time! Got a neat new sun tan, too, I suppose?

Your fine letter of July 19 has arrived, and it was wonderful to hear from you again.

It sounds as if I am going to have some new relations before long. Well, Kath, I think it will be swell! I know you, Neal, Mom and Dad have talked it all over, and you know whatever you decide will be plenty O.K. with me. You know I'd like very much to be at your wedding, but please don't worry about that because it may be quite some time before I get home.

You know, Kath, whatever pleases you, Mom and Dad will please your brother. If you do get married this year please let me know when, so I can do a bit of shopping, etc. You are a peach, honey, and I'm all for anything that makes you happy.

I've been on a pass and had quite an interesting time. I visited a very famous city and did not realize until I returned that I was very close to Margaret's home. I'm almost sure I'll be able to see her one of these days. I'm writing a letter to you, Mother and Dad tonight and will tell more about it then.

Enclosed you will find a little pin that I bought while on pass. Not very much, but it is rather cute, I guess. I've one just like it for Mom, too.

Please say "Hello" to Neal for me, and tell him I'd like very much to meet him. I know he is a good boy because you and the folks like him so well!

Keep well, keep happy, and have fun.

All my love,

Bob.

•————•

August 13, 1944

Dear Mom, Dad and Kath:

Tonight I can write a letter that will be fairly interesting for a change.

On August 11 I went on a 24-hour pass to London. One of the boys from the hut, by the name of Oliver Larson, went with me. We really had a very good time and saw many of the most famous places in the world.

We first went to the Hans Crescent Club, which is just one of the many Red Cross Clubs in London, to get a room for the night. Right here I might say that they are really nice clubs. We could get a bed, meals, snacks, etc. here for quite reasonable prices, which to a soldier's pocket means quite a bit!

I went to the tailor in the club and got my uniform pressed for the first time since I got here. Then we got a real American Coca Cola plus a couple of pieces of cake. Really was awful good! Then we were off to see the city.

We went to Piccadilly Circus which is more like an uptown American city than other sections of the city. Then we saw Trafalgar Square, Nelson's Monument, the Admiralty, Westminster Abbey, and Number 10 Downing Street. In the evening we just rode the subways to different parts of the city, walked about in Hyde Park and the Kensington Gardens, watched soapbox orators by the Serpentine Lake in Hyde Park for quite some time, then walked about until it got so dark we couldn't see our hands in front of our faces. A London blackout is something I will never forget.

About 1 a.m. we finally found our Red Cross Club and had a swell sleep between real sheets.

In the morning of the 12th we hurried out to see more of this great city. We walked down the long beautiful road called "The Mall" to Buckingham Palace. We didn't get to see the change of the guard as they only change every other day. Hope to see it the next time I go there.

Bob in Trafalgar Square in London.

Bob in St. James Park in London.

Bob in front of Buckingham Palace.

We walked all around the palace gardens (outside of course). Really was a long walk, too! Then we walked through St. James Park which is quite pretty. In the afternoon we took the subway to the Holborn Viaduct Station then to the Fenchurch Street Station and walked from there to the Tower of London which is very interesting to see. This old castle is where old Henry VIII had his wives beheaded.

It was getting pretty late in the afternoon when we left the tower so we took a quick look at Tower Bridge and the Thames River and headed for the large Liverpool Street Station, to head back to camp.

In another letter you will find some cards of Westminster Abbey. We took a swell tour through the Abbey and saw many interesting things. I have a rather large book I bought in the Abbey which completely describes it and lists all of the famous people who are buried there. I intend to mail it to you very soon.

I took about 35 snapshots while in London so eventually you will see many of the places I visited. Got some good shots of Big Ben, Buckingham Palace, and many other places. Saw many, many things that I must wait till I get home to tell about. In another envelope will be a map of London on which you can look up the places I mentioned seeing in the letter.

Hope you are all fine and having fun. All for now.

All my love, Bob

.———.

August 26, 1944

Dear Mom and Dad:

In your letter of the 12th, Mom, you assumed that I had been to London. By the time you get this letter you will have received a letter from me telling of my trip to London. However, the city I wrote about, and did not mention the name, was not London. It was another famous city, however. You see, London is the only place we can tell about and mention its name. Other places I visit I cannot send their names to you, but I am keeping them marked on a map so that when I get home I'll be able to tell you about them.

I got a letter from Stanley Clemens today. He is in China now, and the other day he ran into a boy we both knew in basic training at St Petersburg. The same boy went through Truax with me the first time. He was also in Chicago with me. Funny how people who know each other, or know some of the same people the other ones do, will run into each other in such distant lands, isn't it? Just goes to prove that the world isn't so large after all. Old Stan really has done a lot of traveling, hasn't he?

Keep well, keep happy, and have fun.

All my love,

Bob

•————•

August 30, 1944

Dear Mom and Dad:

Congratulations and best wishes on your 20th anniversary, and all the wonderful ones that are yet to come!! Folks, I hope that you had a very, very, happy anniversary. Your plans to celebrate it sound wonderful to me. I sure feel awfully bad because I didn't think of your anniversary in time to send my congratulations when I should have. It seems that I'm almost always late at thinking of events I should never miss.

Gee folks, you sure had a very busy week proceeding Kath's wedding. I know that you both enjoyed it an awful lot, though. Gosh I bet it was a swell wedding and reception. Everything you wrote about sounds wonderful to me, Mother Dear. Mom, I'll bet your cute new hat and dress look wonderful on you!

You know, it's just as I've always said: I've got the most wonderful mom, dad, and sister in the world. I sure do miss you an awful lot!!

Tonight I saw quite a good show. It was an all-girl orchestra from the good old U.S.A., about 7 or 8 girls. It wasn't the best band I've heard by a long shot, but we did have a lot of fun. I don't know when I've laughed as much for a long time. Gee! Sure did have a lot of fun!!

Tomorrow is payday and also shot in the arm day. I hope to go on pass to London again very soon.

Take good care of yourselves and have fun.

Your loving son,

Bob

•———•

September 4, 1944

Dear Mom and Dad:

I just returned from a two-day pass which I spent in London with three of the boys. We really had quite a good time. However, the best of everything was when I got back and found eleven swell letters and a package on my bed. Your letters and the enclosed clippings were swell, the candy was delicious, and I was glad to see the socks and handkerchiefs again. Thanks a million, folks! (By the way, is that the candy Grandma Gay sent or is it from you?) Thanks very, very much to whoever sent it!

You folks wrote wonderful letters describing the wedding, who was there, and of the fine preparations. I believe I can almost picture how everything looked. It must have been a wonderful wedding, and I'll bet that reception was really perfect!!

It was very nice of Sally Napper, her sister, Mrs. Prideaux and Jack's wife to help so much. I'm sure glad that Uncle Alvin got there in time. He really had quite a trip! Hope his pictures are good. I'll bet Aunt Patton was awfully happy to see Kath married to a boy like Neal. Gee, Mom, I'll bet you had the house looking like a million dollars. I'd have given an awful lot to have been there for the whole affair but I'm very glad Kath is married and so very happy. I'd sure be a lot happier if I could have gotten her a wedding present. Do you think I should wait until I get home, or do you think if I turned over $100.00 worth of war bonds it would be O.K.? Would she like that as well as a nice gift? Wish I knew what to do!

The clippings you sent of the wedding are wonderful! Wasn't it swell that you found that nice article on it in the Milwaukee paper! I've got quite a well-known sister and brother-in-law, haven't I!

I'll bet Kath's rings look beautiful. Hope it won't be so very long till I can see them myself. It really is swell that you got to see the State Fair, etc. The Houslets must have some fine horses alright! Glad they are winning so many races.

While in London this time I went to Madam Tussaud's Wax Museum. It is, I believe, the most interesting of the many places I saw in London. There are wax models of scores of famous people living of this century and others. They are so good that if the living man were to stand beside the model it would be practically impossible to tell the model from the man. Really is almost unbelievable that they can be so perfect. There are quite a few famous Americans there, also Hitler and his boys. Quite a place!

We also went to an English play that has been going for four years and ends this week. It was very good. The name of the play was "Quiet Week End." The Red Cross told us to be sure to see it as it was really full of English humor. They were absolutely right!

Well folks, I'm very happy to know that you folks are enjoying everything and that Kath is so happy. I think you gave her a wonderful wedding that will always be a beautiful memory for all of you.

Take good care of yourselves and have all the fun you can. Time to hit the sack for a few hours now, folks, so good night for tonight.

All my love,
Bob

·———·

September 8, 1944

Dear Mom and Dad:

Another cool, stormy day that has been very dull in every way. The weather here is so damp and cool that it actually feels colder than it does when we have four feet of snow at home. We have been issued some nice warm fleece lined leather pants and jackets, though, so we can keep nice and warm just the same. We keep a fire in our stove during the evening if we can find enough wood to burn, still do not need a fire during the day-light hours as yet.

My cold is all better so I really do feel fine and I hope you folks are feeling the best ever.

We are getting along quite well. Plenty to eat (not in any way comparable to real cooking, but we get along it O.K.) and plenty of sleep these days.

Oh yes, thanks for the Dewey button, Dad. It caused a real commotion! Really had a lot of fun with it!

Well, folks, have fun and give my best to everyone.

Good night,

Love Bob

P.S. Enclosed is one shoulder patch you asked for Dad, also an Underground or subway ticket from London.

·———·

September 12, 1944

Dear Mom and Dad:

Your letter of September 10 came today, Mom. I really enjoyed it very much. Kath is really getting along fine for such a new housewife, isn't she! Dad, you better send Kath the secret of making those colored pancakes. I'll bet that would cause quite a commotion in Oxford! Holy smokes! Those kids sure are having a big time aren't they! I'm mighty happy for them. What a swell pair! I'm glad Yippee is enjoying herself so much. I'll bet she has plenty of room to play in now.

Oh yes, I've got the pictures that were taken at Kearns, Utah all labeled and ready to send home. They are the ones that you sent me a couple of months ago, Mom. My pictures that I took here should be developed and returned to me in a few days now. I'll send them to you as soon as they get back from London.

Folks, do you think it would be alright for me to drop my war bond and have a voluntary allotment of about thirty or forty dollars sent home instead? You see they just take out whatever amount I designate each month and send it home in cash. That way I'd have a bit of ready money in the bank when I get home. I doubt it I will be able to cash the bonds for a while after the war because I know the government couldn't cash everyone's at once. I figured I might be able to use some money when I get home for clothes, etc. I actually believe I would be able to send more home in cash to be put in the bank than I'm putting away by bonds. What do you think about it?

Well, I guess I'd better get to bed now as I have to be up at 0600 in the morning tomorrow. I hope you are fine and having fun, folks. Say "Hello" to Ed and Connie for me.

So long for tonight, all my love,

Bob

.———.

September 16, 1944

Dearest Mom and Dad:

Last night I had a swell dream about the wonderful times we used to have. Gee, but we were lucky!

I can fool around, laugh, and keep busy, but gosh! I sure do miss you folks, Kath, home, and the old gang, etc.!! I just dream of the day when I can come home and live that wonderful life once again.

Either you or Mom once asked me if your letters to me are censored or not. Well, they are not censored.

Not much news today that I can write about but maybe tomorrow I can do better.

Give my best to everyone and keep happy and well! I'm fine and all is O.K.

All my love,

Bob.

P.S. Please stick a pocket comb in the next letter or two. Lost mine today. Thank you!

.———.

September 22, 1944

Dearest Mom and Dad:

Tonight it is raining quite hard after a fairly nice day. The old rain really makes a lot of noise on these metal huts. Kind of restful though! I'm now quite well acquainted with English fog, too!

Believe me when I tell you that it is all that you've ever read about it! Really gets plenty soupy here at times.

I hope you are enjoying some well fall weather. Gee, it won't be long till Thanksgiving Day! Only a couple more months now. Hope you go to Grandma Lee's just as we always have done. Maybe Kath and Neal would like to go there, too. I know Grandma would love that!

There just isn't anything I can write about, folks, so I hope you won't mind if I cut this rather short tonight. I hope you are both feeling real good and that you're having a lot of fun!! Guess I'll get a bit of good old sleep now, so good night, Mom and Pop. I'll write again tomorrow or Sunday. I'm fine and everything is okey doke!!

All my love,

Bob

P.S. Enclosed is a list of exhibits that I saw at Madame Tussaud's in London. A wonderful exhibit of wax models of famous people. A world-famous place.

·———·

September 30, 1944

Dearest Mom and Dad:

Thanks a lot for the swell letters of the 19th and 20th of September I got one from each of you, plus a news bulletin from Pop. That was quite a clipping you sent to me Dad. How they get all the information is more than I can see. The paper was correct in stating that the date as August 1943. You see, the whole division was cited and as the citation was just given out after we were members of this division we received the citation, too. Our group is in for the same citation by itself and when it comes

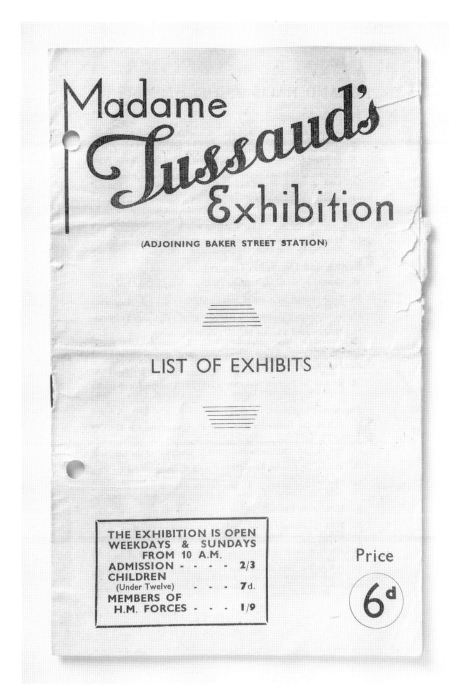

Madame Tussaud's brochure from Bob's visit.

through we will wear an Oak Leaf Cluster on our ribbons. It usually takes eight to twelve months for a citation of this kind to come through. Thanks again for the clipping, dad. Pop, I'm glad that everything is going so well for you. Hope you can get plenty of help.

Well, Mom and Dad, I guess that's about all for tonight. This war isn't over yet, and in my opinion it won't be for quite some time. Longer than most people think. Believe me when I tell you that the Germans haven't lost their punch as yet!!!

I'm awfully glad you are feeling so well and having so much fun. I'm fine and okey doke!

So long for today, all my love,
Bob

·———·

October 3, 1944

Dearest Mom and Dad:

Mom, you and Dad really have a wonderful idea about a gift to Kath, from me. I think those blankets will be wonderful!! Thanks a million for suggesting it to me! You'll find the nice card you sent me, to include with the blankets, enclosed here in. I hope I did a good job in writing it. You folks sure are wonderful! The best Mom and Dad a guy could ever have!!!

Mom dear, you really did your good deed for the day when you found that soldier's wife and baby such a fine place to live.

I really enjoyed reading the list of gifts that Kath and Neal received. They really have got a marvelous collection of things. Everyone was very generous to them. They are two awfully lucky kids!!

Guess that's all for now so, so long for now.
All my love,
Bob

P.S. Some more of those dandy cookies, etc. would taste awfully good! Thanks ever so much!

————

October 7, 1944

Dearest Mom and Dad:

Thanks a million for the swell picture of Kath, Neal, Marge, Mary Ellen, Best Man, wedding cake, etc. It came out very well, didn't it. Gosh, but they look swell! It really is a peach of a picture! Or as they would say over here; "It's a pip"! Oh yes, the dining room sure looks swell, Mom.

It was very interesting to hear all about Kath and Neal, Mom. And I must say that the banana cream pie, you mentioned that Kath made, sounds awfully good!! I'll bet she will become a wonderful cook just like you are Mom! I'm anxiously waiting more of the fine pictures of Kath's wedding and more of Uncle Alvin's kids.

Weather here is quite cold now, but am keeping plenty warm just the same. I feel fine and everything is O.K. I'm still holding out against the colds around here O.K.

Keep well, keep happy and have fun.

Love, Bob

————

October 10, 1944

Dearest Mom and Dad:

Good morning! Hope you are feeling swell. Better brace yourselves for a big surprise!

Enclosed is a money order for $80.00. I'd appreciate it very, very much if you would use whatever amount of it you need to do my Xmas shopping for me. There is hardly anything to buy over here so I believe this will be the best way for me to get it done. *Please* use this money so I'll feel sort of like I'd done a little something for Xmas. Please be sure to get Kath and Neal, the Grandmas, Grandpas and cousins all fixed up right. Don't forget the Sasmans. Sometime soon I am going to London again to see what I can do. Might be able to find something.

Oh yes, Mom, take out the cost of those nice blankets I'm giving to Kath and Neal, too. I know you will do a far better job at buying the presents than I could do. Please don't think I've forgotten my Mom and Dad!! Thanks from the bottom of my heart! You're wonderful!

All my love,

Bob

.———————.

October 23, 1944

Dearest Mom and Dad:

[First paragraph of six lines cut out by censor because of paragraph written on other side of sheet.]

...of the time the past few weeks.

We are getting along all right though. Plenty warm and dry most of the time as we have pretty good clothes.

Well, folks, I feel fine, keep fairly busy, and everything is okey doke. We still... [Six lines cut out by censor.]

Listened to a swell program on the radio direct from the States today. Really sounded good! In fact, last week I listened to the actual broadcast of the Wisconsin-Ohio State football game from the good old stadium in Madison, Wis.! That really was a thrill! Just to think that I could hear people yelling and cheering just about one mile from home! The game was broadcast over the A.F.N. (American Forces Network) at 8:45 p.m. British Summer Time. We heard from three minutes before the half to the end of the game.

Well, Mom and Dad, take good care of yourselves and have fun! Time to get to bed so—

Good night folks,

All my love,

Bob.

.———————.

October 25, 1944

Dearest Mom and Dad:

Yesterday, I got a nice letter from Red Clemens. It only took around 17 days to get here from China. Not bad is it?

Mom, those snapshots of Kath and Neal, and the family and friends by the church are *wonderful*! Thanks very much for sending them to me. I noticed Edith in the snapshot by the church and she certainly looks wonderful! Very pretty young lady.

Kath and Neal look extremely happy. They look like a fine-looking pair! Everyone looks very, very nice.

I know Kath will love those blankets. You are wonderful to think up those swell ideas, Mom!

I'll bet you would enjoy hearing us argue over the election. Boy! What times do we have! Sounds worse than the Chicago Stock Exchange. I'm really hard at it though and am sure plugging Dewey for all I am worth. I sure would like to see him win!

Well, folks, time for me to get my beauty rest so will say "Good night" for today.

Keep well and happy, and please don't work too hard.

All my love,

Bob.

.———.

October 30, 1944

Dearest Mom and Dad:

Mom, the picture of the dining room, on the morning after Kath's wedding, really looks good! Everything looks just like it did when I last saw it. Sure will be a great day when I get to see it again!

I got the box with the good candy and Nabiscos, plus the swell hankies. Can use them as I have lost a few in the laundry. Thank you very, very much!

I got two nice letters from Kath today telling me all about their good times, etc. She certainly is pleased with the living room set

Bob with one of his buddies.

and vacuum cleaner that Gay Bros. gave them. They are sure
happy & I'm glad they have gained weight. Kath's cooking must
be pretty good.

Yes, Mom, that piece of wedding cake was very good. It was
still fresh and very good and tasty!

Congratulations on your U.S.O. award, Mom. You certainly do
deserve far more than that for all the good work you have done!

Guys around the huts.

Say, Dad, Mom tells me you now have a real good-looking girl on one of the elevators? That's the boy, Pop! Keep things looking plenty neat!

Take it easy, keep well, and have fun.

All my love,

Bob

P.S. Thanks again for the swell letters, packages, etc.

.————.

November 4, 1944

Dearest Mom and Dad:

I'm glad to know that you received the Kearns pictures and the one of Hallman, Cuddyer, and myself. No, Mom, there is no street light at the end of our hut. That pole is to hold the wires for our lights in the hut. There are just a couple of long winding country roads going through the camp. No streets at all. We still keep black out regulations each night.

Mom, you're a pretty good guesser on that historical sight I mentioned seeing. [Note from Mom: That was the Air-borne Army taking off from his base for Holland.]

Yes, Mom, I saw the University you mentioned. [Note from Mom: That was the University at Cambridge when he visited there.]

Gee, it will be swell to see old Norwood Place again! Walestads live about thirty miles south of there. [Note from Mom: That was to tell us that he is thirty miles south of Norwich.]

Oh yes, I'm glad you came pretty close to first place in your contest, Mom. You are very clever, Mom! [Note from Mom: He is referring to the way I was able to ask him and find out where he is.] Keep up the good work. Those guessing contests are a lot of fun aren't they?

Guess I never did tell you much about our huts. They are about fifteen feet wide and thirty-five feet long. They are made of corrugated steel and have Congoleum floors. We have one small stove in the center of the hut and two windows in each end. There is a back door, a front door, and one more door directly in line with and about five feet inside the front door. This enables us to go outside the hut at night with the hut lights on, without showing any light. There are sixteen of us in this hut.

Well, folks, I guess that's about all for today. I'm fine, growing quite a beard these days, and still say "There's no place like home!" I hope you are both well and happy. Take good care of yourselves, have fun, and give my best to all.

All my love,
Bob

·———·

November 7, 1944

Dearest Mom and Dad:

I got a fine letter from Kath written on October 23. She called me Grandpa just as you said she would. It seems that I have referred to them as "kids" several times. They really made it clear to me that they are a young married couple but not "kids." More fun!!

I enjoyed the newspaper clippings about the homecoming game, etc. very much!

How's everything with you, Dad? Going along swell I hope! Keeping plenty busy as usual I imagine.

How's your back this fall, Mom? Don't work too hard and hurt it again, will you. That's the stuff! I'm fine and keeping busy. Not much news today.

All my love,
Bob

P.S. I got my fingers crossed for Dewey tonight!

·———·

November 15, 1944

Dearest Mom and Dad:

Some of my Xmas packages have arrived. Today, I got three packages, one from the Rues, one from Uncle Alvin and Aunt Lillian, and one from Nappers. It certainly was awfully nice of all of them to remember me in such a swell way.

I imagine the kids—oh oh! I mean Kath and Neal are enjoying life as much as ever. I've got to remember not to call them "kids," after my lecture from Kath.

We are listening to Bob Hope tonight. His program is coming over the A.F.N. which is about the only station over here worth listening to. It is the American Forces Network over which we hear American programs, music, news, etc. Really makes us feel pretty close to home to be able to hear things just like we did at home.

Hope you have a wonderful Thanksgiving Day, folks. Wish I could be with you.

All my love,
Bob

•———•

November 16, 1944

Dearest Mom and Dad:

I'm glad to hear that you are so well and having so much fun.

You folks sound pretty busy these days with work, U.S.O., Red Cross, Kath and Neal, etc. Glad you are having a good time. Your letters are real interesting, Mom dear. Wish I could write some that could be as good. I think you made quite a buy on that toaster, Mom. I got a big kick out of that. Nice work!!

Sorry to hear that Jack McCann is missing. Hope he will turn up O.K.

It is good to hear that Kath is continuing her painting. I'll bet she will turn out some beauties of her horses, etc.

Thanks again for all the good news, etc. Keep well and happy, and have fun!!

All my love,
Bob.

•———•

Same Ol' Place
November 19, 1944

Dearest Mom and Dad:

I just returned from the show "Home in Indiana." It was wonderful!! I could just picture Kath all through the show. It sure was a honey!

Your plans and ideas about selling the house and building a new one sound swell. You letter telling me all the dope about things is a honey, Dad.

I sure had to laugh when I pictured all the junk etc. that you must have hauled out of the basement. I'll bet the kids going to Dudgeon School had a regular field day helping themselves to the stuff.

Yes, folks, I really am quite excited about the whole idea. I know how much you have wanted to build for a long time. Now you will be able to put all of your ideas about improving the different parts of the house together—and out will come a wonderful new home. As to where we should build, I'm a bit partial towards Nakoma. The main thing is to stay well out on Madison's West Side, don't you agree??

Well, Mom and Dad, I guess I'm about due to hit the old bunk for a while so better say "Good night."

All my love,
Bob

P.S. Have received several packages lately and am saving them until Christmas.

·————·

November 27, 1944

Dearest Mom and Dad:

I'm sorry I've not written to you for the past three days. I've been extra busy working, and taking my turn at guard duty.

It was interesting to hear about your conversation with Miss Brown. Almost believe I can remember delivering groceries to her when I worked for Nappers.

No, Mom, we never get K.P. anymore, but we do have inspection twice a week. They aren't bad at all.

I was glad to hear all about Melvin. That boy really gets around! Glad he sent that rupee for our book. We, too, have eaten dehydrated foods of all kinds, but now get fresh stuff for the most part. I believe, so far as foods are concerned, that I miss having a good old glass of cold milk most of all.

Dad, the plan you drew of our new apartment really looks good. You and Mom will have it looking like a million dollars. Wherever you and Mom are living is home sweet home to me! I'd sure love to help you move but I'm afraid I just couldn't talk the C.O. into a little vacation just now. I'm awfully glad everything is coming along so well. Hope you can get the price you want for the house.

I'm feeling plenty O.K. and raring to get home again, just like all the others here.

Keep well and happy,
All my love,
Bob.

.———————.

December 1, 1944

Dearest Mom and Dad:

I'm awfully sorry I didn't get a letter off to you yesterday as I intended. Just didn't get a chance to write.

Gee, the packages are really rolling in! Don't hardly know where to put all of them. Everyone certainly is good to me! I'm saving the packages till Christmas.

I haven't had any letters from you for a few days now. I guess the Xmas packages are taking up most of the shipping space. Our hut is stacked full of packages. Sure looks great!!

We had good weather the last couple of days as you will be able to tell by the newspapers. The heavies really went out in force.

Enclosed you will find a few snap shots and the negatives. They were the pictures I took of the troop laden C-47 cargo planes towing gliders on their way to Holland during the invasion late September. When you have them enlarged you will be able to see them much better. The sky was actually loaded with planes. It was really a sight to remember!

Planes towing gliders.

Planes towing gliders.

Planes towing gliders.

Well Mom and Dad, I hope you are feeling just swell, have sold the house, and are having lots of fun.

I'm fine, no cold or anything.

All for now, all my love,

Bob

·———·

December 7, 1944

Dearest Mom and Dad:

Sorry for the delay in my writing but I have been on a two-day pass in London. I have had a swell time! The best pass I have had since I have been here. Harold Yoke, of Elwood, Indiana, and I went together. We saw a couple of fine shows, and went to a wonderful dance in one of the largest ball rooms I have ever seen. It was in the old London Opera House that was burned in the 1800s and then rebuilt. There were around 4,000 people there, and there are dances there every afternoon and night of the week. The attendance is always huge; two good bands—an all-girl band and an all-male band. Really is quite a place. The place is now called the "Covert Gardens."

I met a very nice, beautiful, blue-eyed, blonde Norwegian girl. She is in the Norske Marines and is stationed in London at the present time. I'll probably never see her again, but she certainly was a swell girl! Really nice girl!!! One afternoon I talked about an hour with a Norwegian officer. He hasn't seen any of his family for over five years. He was an interesting man. All told, I had a fine pass!

Now to answer your letters that came while I was on pass. It sure is wonderful to come in and find letters from you on my bed. I'm awfully happy to hear that you sold the house. You did a fine job! It was good to hear about your evening at the Sherlocks'. How did you like the rabbit?

Gee, the more I hear about the new apartment, and think about our new house, the more excited I get about it all. Everything is certainly going along well! It sounds like a mighty nice little apartment. Sure won't have far to go for coffee cake, etc. More fun!! Glad to hear about the room for my electric train—sure got a laugh when I thought about that, Dad.

My watch still runs, I'm getting a new crystal made as I broke the other one.

Glad to hear that you are playing those big rummy games. Glad that Jack McCann is alive. I'm glad that you and Dad like my bed so well. Really is a good ol' bed!! No Mom, I didn't hear the Win.-Minn. game, but I got a swell letter from Carole Rue telling me all about it. She certainly is becoming a regular young lady. I've been intending to send you something from here as a Christmas present. I just can't find anything worth sending, have looked around here and in London but no luck so far. I'm afraid I won't find anything in time for Xmas now so wanted you to know that I've tried. I'm very, very sorry that I haven't made out better.

Take good care of yourselves, have fun, and don't work too hard! Have a very Merry Christmas and a Happy New Year!!!

All my love,
Bob

·————·

December 15, 1944

Dear Mom and Dad,

Today I received my first letter from our new home. Your letter was swell, Mom. Thanks a million.

I'm glad you received these fifteen pamphlets. Those letters sure took a long time to come to you, didn't they?

I'm glad you are all settled so nicely in the new apartment. Everything sounds swell! Gee, I can hardly wait to get home. We sure live close to the bakery, grocery store, barber, drug store, etc. Will be fun to get up in the morning and hop down to the bakery for coffee cake, etc. Well folks, time to chow—will write again tomorrow. Keep well and have fun!

All my love,
Bob

·————·

December 19, 1944

Dear Mom and Dad:

After a two-week delay in all mail service, except for V-Mail, we all got a nice pile of letters. It certainly boosted everyone's morale a lot to see all that wonderful mall! You can hardly imagine how good it makes me feel to hear from you. I'll always remember how good it feels to get such swell letters.

Lloyd Pullen is really up close to the Jerries, isn't he! Also am glad to know where Kath's brother is. Sounds like a very rainy place. He hasn't so much on us so far as rain and fog are concerned.

Folks, I really enjoyed that wonderful composite letter from everyone at the Sasmans' party. It was very nice of everyone concerned to write such nice notes to me. We sure had a swell bunch of neighbors didn't we. Anyway we still live plenty close so can see them as often as ever. It was swell of the Sasmans to have that swell surprise party for you. Glad everyone had so much fun. Please thank everyone for those notes, Mom and Dad. They made me feel very, very good.

I'm very happy that everything is in such fine shape for I'm feeling darn good and hope you folks are feeling even better than that. Take good care of yourselves and have fun. Thanks again for all your wonderful letters. Good night, Mom and Dad.

All my love,
Bob

·———·

December 24, 1944

Dear Mom and Dad:

Here it is the day before Christmas and the most beautiful day we have had for weeks. The sky is clear blue and the sun is shining. It really is a fine day!!

It certainly doesn't seem like Christmas around here except for the piles of packages on the shelves over our beds. Some snow sure would help.

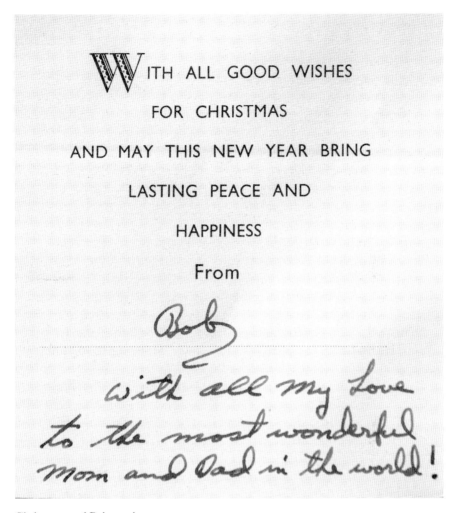

WITH ALL GOOD WISHES

FOR CHRISTMAS

AND MAY THIS NEW YEAR BRING

LASTING PEACE AND

HAPPINESS

From

Bob

with all my Love to the most wonderful Mom and Dad in the world!

Christmas card Bob sent home.

Pop, you sure are meeting a lot of new girls aren't you! Just keep those elevators going, Dad. Are any blonds running them now? Or is this the redheads week? More fun!!

I enjoyed reading that letter from Kath. Hope her side is alright. She certainly is having a wonderful time! I'll bet she is a dandy cook—she should be after watching you cook so long, Mom!

Glad you received those Christmas tags, Mom. Hope I fixed 'em up O.K. I'm glad you had such a fine time at the Past Matrons Club dinner party. I also am happy to know that my letters are reaching you O.K. Hope they don't take too long to get there.

I hope you are fine and having a swell time! I'll be thinking of you extra hard tonight and tomorrow. Hope you have a wonderful Christmas!!!!

All my love,
Bob

·———·

Wednesday, December 27, 1944

Dear Mom and Dad:

Thanks, thanks a million for all the swell things you sent for Christmas. I can sure use everything you sent! Everyone was very good to me!!

I got many fine gifts from you, Uncle Dave, Jackie, Nappers, Uncle John and Aunt Maude, Uncle Alvin and family, Sasmans, Grandma Lee, Grandma Gay (in the bank), Grandma Montgomery, Kath and Neal, Uncle Harley and family, and the Sherlock family.

I got lots of swell stationery, candy, cookies, cheese, cocoa, marshmallows, fruit cake, etc. We really are eating good! Now for the many fine things other than food. First of all, Mom and Dad, that "University of Wisconsin" sweatshirt is a honey! Boy, can I ever use that! And those socks and handkerchiefs are swell, too! Oh yes, those plaid socks certainly are neat. We all got a big kick out of those! I'll wear 'em, too! Bet you had plenty to do with those, Pop!

Then those books are mighty nice to have, also. Those humor books of yours, the crossword puzzle book, the book *Sad Sack* from Uncle Dave and family, and the good book by Bob Hope from Grandma Montgomery! I will write to each and everyone in the very near future to thank them for their very fine presents. ALL WAS SWELL!!!!

This is a Christmas I shall always remember! I worked all day on the 24ᵗʰ plus all that night. We had plenty of business to tend to Christmas Eve. When I got back to the hut about 8:30 a.m.

How Bob kept track of Christmas thank-you letters (*top*) and who he sent Christmas cards to (*bottom*).

on Christmas, I didn't go to bed cause it was Christmas and a beautiful day.

Everything was covered with thick white frost! The ground and trees were beautiful!! We had a pretty good dinner (menu enclosed) and took in the movie on the base in the p.m. I finally hit the old sack about 9:30 p.m. I was a bit sleepy by then.

I hope you had a wonderful Christmas, Mom and Dad. I'm anxious to hear about it! I'm terribly sorry I didn't get something for you but I'll find something eventually, I hope!!!!

I'm feeling very, very fine and hope you feel even better than that!

Happy New Year, Mom and Dad!!!

Your loving son,

Bob

•———•

December 31, 1944

Dear Mom and Dad:

Sorry I have not written for the past few days. We have been quite busy as you no doubt have heard over the radio. Old Adolph has been getting plenty this Christmas season. He'll get plenty more, too!! You can bet on that!!

I'll certainly be a busy boy in my spare time for a while now, as I have better than twenty-two letters to answer plus my thank-you notes for the nice things I received for Christmas. I've certainly been lucky with my mail the past two days. Everyone is mighty good to me!!

Mom and Dad, I want you to know that I appreciate your wonderful letters more than it is possible to express in words. They are always so full of news about the things that interest me most of all. You are the most wonderful Mom and Dad in the world!!

Mom and Dad, I'm sorry you worried so much about what I might think about your selling the house. I wish I would have cabled you my consent right away. I figured you might get my letters much faster than you did. I am very, very happy about the

Dec. 31, 1944
Sunday P.M.

Dear Mom and Dad:

Sorry I have not written for the past few days. We have been quite busy as you no doubt have heard over the radio. Old Adolph has been getting plenty this Christmas Season. He'll get plenty more, too!! You can bet on that!!

I'll certainly be a busy boy in my spare time for awhile now, as I have better than twenty-two letters to answer plus my thank-you notes for the nice things I received for Christmas. I've certainly been lucky with my mail the past two days. I have a neat pile of swell letters dating from November 18th. to Dec. 19th. Really complete coverage! I have lots of wonderful letters from you, and others from Kath, Aunt Ruth, Uncle John and Aunt Maude, Grandma Gay, Grandma Lee, Uncle Dave, Bob Sasman, Jackie, and Donald Berger. Also nice Christmas cards from Hanneman's, Prideaux's, Oscars, etc. Everyone is mighty good to me!!

Mom and Dad, I want you to know that I appreciate your wonderful letters more than it is possible to express in words. They are always so full of news about the things that interest me most of all. You are the most wonderful Mom and Dad in the world!!

I was glad to know that you had such a grand time with Aunt Mable, Uncle Bernice, and Grandma and Grandpa Montgomery. Also, thank you for Harvey's address. I've put it in my book. Might run into him sometime--never can tell.

Oh yes, Mom, I'll get some shoulder patches and send them to you right away. Sorry I didn't get your letter about them earlier, just got it yesterday. I promised Hazel one so will send it directly to her. O.K.? Hope so! Mom, the next time I go on pass I'll try to find some more of those little Air Force pins. I'll get a few and send them to you.

Mom and Dad, I'm sorry you worried so much about what I might think about your selling the house. I wish I would have cabled you my consent right away. I figured you might get my letters much faster than you did. I am very, very happy about the deal. Besides, Mom and Dad, you should know that I'm all for anything you do as I always know it is the right thing!! And Mom, don't ever worry about the way you write to me. I love it! If you want to tell me I'm staying out too late, or anything else like that when I get home, you go right ahead and do it!!

Oh yes, I also want you to know that we now have hot water for shaving and showers at certain hours of th[...] Pretty nice, eh?

Mom, you asked me to send some requests. I should after all those swell packages I received However, I would like to have a good watch strap, cookies, etc. Guess it would be better to send th[...] letter or first-class mail. Regular men's strap s[...] watch O.K.

Golly Mom, you sure are working at the U.S.O. a lot. It really is awfully nice of you Mom. Glad you are having so much fun. Please don't work too hard, though!

I'm very, very sorry to hear that Lloyd Pullen was killed. He was a swell guy. In fact, I don't think anyone was ever liked more than Lloyd was. It must be a bad blow to Lois Baker. They were engaged, I believe.

I also am very sorry to hear that Jackie is divorced. She has always kept writing to me from time to time, and I gathered a while back that things weren't going very well for her. She is a swell girl, and I'm sorry things didn't turn out better for her. She has never said just what happened, so I'm very much puzzled about the whole thing. Hope Jean Lee feels better about it now. Guess it couldn't be helped.

You really have a nice collection of Christmas cards, haven't you? Pretty nice for our book, Mom!

Yes, I know Bob Sasman has a new girl friend that he really thinks the world of. Every time he writes to me he raves about her. She sounds like a peach!

Mom, thanks again for all the Christmas shopping you did for me. It was swell of you!

Dad, did you get to see Mom walk around with the candle at Eastern Star? Bet it was quite the thing, eh! Sorry Don Williams is sick. Hope he will be O.K. soon. Glad Harry Stoll is home on furlough. Hope he gets his discharge from this army soon! The new door system on the building sounds like a good idea, Dad. How is it working? Also was glad to get Aunt Maudes and Uncle John's address in St. Petersburg, Fla., Dad. Glad to hear that the house deal is closed and all is set. Makes a nice pile of bonds folks, Mighty Nice!! The new apartment sounds swell! I can hardly wait to see it. Boy oh Boy! Will I be glad to get home again folks! Hope it wont be too long now!

Weather here is cold now, even had a bit of snow today. The roads are icy from thick white frosts. Glad you are both so well! Keep it up! I'm feeling plenty O.K. and things here go on as usual.

Mom dear, thanks for that wonderful Christmas kiss. I sent plenty to you in my thoughts.

Dad, thanks for all the swell clippings and bulletins you have sent. They are interesting to see. Must seem nice not to have any sidewalk to shovel, etc. Hope the P-12 is running O.K.!

It was swell of you to send those snaps to Campbell's folks and Larison's wife, Mom. They want me to thank you for them. So "Thanks" Mom!

This is New Years Eve, now, so----HAPPY NEW YEAR MOM AND DAD!!!! Hope we will be together next year at this time!

All my love,
Bob.

Bob's New Year's Eve
letter home.

deal. Besides, Mom and Dad, you should know that I'm all for anything you do as I always know it is the right thing!!

And Mom, don't ever worry about the way you write to me. I love it! If you want to tell me I'm staying out too late, or anything else like that when I get home, you go right ahead and do it!!

Oh yes, I also want you to know that we now have hot water for shaving and showers at certain hours of the day. Pretty nice, eh?

Mom, you asked me to send some requests. I hardly think I should after all those swell packages I received for Christmas. However, I would like to have a good watch strap, and always like cookies, etc. Guess it would be better to send the strap in a letter or first-class mail. Regular men's strap should fit the watch O.K.

Golly Mom, you sure are working at the U.S.O. a lot. It really is awfully nice of you Mom. Please don't work too hard, though! Glad you are having so much fun.

I'm very, very sorry to hear that Lloyd Pullen was killed. He was a swell guy. In fact, I don't think anyone was ever liked more than Lloyd was. It must be a bad blow to Lois Baker. They were engaged, I believe.

Dad, did you get to see Mom walk around with the candle at Eastern Star? Bet it was quite the thing, eh!

The new apartment sounds swell! I can hardly wait to see it. Boy oh boy! Will I be glad to get home again folks! Hope it won't be too long now!

Mom dear, thanks for that wonderful Christmas kiss. I sent plenty to you in my thoughts.

This is New Year's Eve, now, SO—HAPPY NEW YEAR MOM AND DAD!!!! Hope we will be together next year at this time.

All my love,

Bob

.———.

January 4, 1945

Dear Mom and Dad:

I'm very glad to know that you got our gifts off to the uncles, aunts, grandmas and grandpas and cousins in plenty of time so they received them for Christmas. Mom dear, you really did a perfect job of Christmas shopping for me. I know Kath, Barbara, and everyone else will like what you chose for me. Thanks very, very much Mom!!

Dad, your letter of December 21 was swell. I got a big kick reading all about your activities of that day. It should be titled: "My Day—by Len Gay!" You sure do keep hopping just like always, don't you! It was fun hearing about the Martins, and Russ Slightum. Please say "Hello" to Russ, Mr. Martin and Jerry Coulter for me. I'm awfully glad everything about the house is completed and all O.K.

Mom and Dad, thanks from the very bottom of my heart for your swell Christmas presents to me. That money will be a dandy thing to have when I get home. You really shouldn't have done it! I hope you used some of the money I sent home to buy those Christmas presents with! All the Christmas I wanted was to be very certain I knew that my Mom and Dad were well and happy!! It is just as I have always said: there aren't any words that can express what a wonderful Mom and Dad I have!!!

I'm feeling plenty O.K., and things here are O.K. We are plenty busy these days.

Keep well and happy!! Good night Mom and Dad,

All my love,

Bob

⋅———⋅

January 9, 1945

Dear Mom and Dad:

I hope the space between my letters to you won't be too long. I haven't written for a few days as I was quite busy and then went on pass for two days besides. I went to London by myself this trip and really had a fine time. I just got back last night and found a huge stack of wonderful letters on my bed. It sure makes me feel swell to get so many dandy letters! Besides that when I got up about 6 o'clock this morning and opened the door I saw some beautiful white snow! Everything is covered with about two inches of nice fluffy snow. They claim it is the heaviest snow in these parts for years. Anyhow, it sure made me think of home. All of us boys from the North were awfully glad to see snow but the southern boys just couldn't get excited about it. It is cold and icy right now. Not as cold nor as much snow as you have there but real winter weather for England!

Glad you gave Uncle Dave and Don the bow and arrow. Hope they have fun with them. Glad you saved my golf set, train, rifle, etc. I hope to have a son to give my electric train to someday. If he will have as much fun with it as I did when I was a little fella it will be well worth saving. It's a swell little train! I'm awfully glad you have been using my toilet articles. I know I had a lot of stuff laying around and am glad you can use it.

I'm not sure just how much I weigh, Mom. Will weigh myself when I next go to town. Will guess about 170—174 lbs. I'm not sure about my shoe size any more. Believe my foot is a little wider than it was—no longer though!

Boy oh boy, Dad, you may not hear as many stories as you used to from Chuck, Sam, Chet, and Joe, but I sure hear plenty to make up for them. The boys bring in some rare stories every now and then. Real killer-dillers!!! Glad Lars and Ed are still working for you, Dad. Guess that raise made them plenty happy, eh! Oh yes, Pop! Thanks very much for the pocket calendars. We can use them.

Mom, you did a perfectly magnificent job of buying Christmas presents for everyone from me. You described each present so well to me that I just know everyone was delighted with their gifts. And Mom dear, you did a perfect job of wrapping them. Those sample stickers you sent are swell! You did a perfect job, Mom! Just as I knew you would do!

I just received another box of swell Toll House cookies and Divinity candy from Grandma Lee and Aunt Oly. What delicious stuff! Yum yum!!

Glad you are well and having fun!

All my love,

Bob

•———•

January 13, 1945

Dear Mom and Dad:

It is swell to know that you had such a swell time on New Year's Eve, Mom and Dad! Folks, guess you might as well give that bottle of champagne to Lars also.—That is unless you want it? (Joke.)

I'm glad to hear that Don Oscar made sgt. He has done alright for himself!

Mom, you asked about my oxfords. However, I don't want to trouble you about such things as that. I can get shoes over here O.K! They are nice oxfords and altho they will cost about 3 pounds or $12.00 it will be best, I believe, I will be fitted right. You see, I'm not sure just what size oxford I wear now and the English sizes run a bit different. Use that shoe stamp for yourselves. O.K.? Hope so!!!

Mom dear, it was wonderful to hear all about your Christmas with Kath and Neal. I'm awfully happy that you and Dad were with them and that you had such a fine time! Also am glad Bob Kurtenacker is back in Chicago. I got a swell Christmas card from him with a picture of the baby on it. Little Bobbie sure is cute!

Mom and Dad, thank God you didn't ride that train that was wrecked, as you had planned!!

You folks sure did work hard getting moved. Only wish I could have helped! Thanks again, Mom and Dad, for all your wonderful newsy letters! I'm fine and everything is O.K! Take care of yourselves and have fun!

Your loving son,
Bob

·————·

January 18, 1945

Dear Mom and Dad:

I'm glad everything at home is so swell! Wish we could have some nice dry, sparkling snow around here. Our little wet snow only lasted a couple of days or so.

I'm terrible [*sic*] sorry to hear that Bob Dixon was killed. He was a real guy! One of Pepper's very good pals, too. It was good to hear that Don and Ruth Ann liked their Christmas gifts so well. You are a swell Santa Claus, Mom!

We had a big inspection here yesterday. This base is really cleaned up now. Everyone, except a very light crew to keep the base in operation, had to stand inspection on one of the runways. A major general (2 stars) and a brigadier general (1 star) plus a pile of colonels, etc. did the inspecting. Luckily I had to work so didn't have to stand it. I was all ready for the inspection, except for changing into my O.D. uniform, when our planes returned to the base. They called for four of us and I was one of the lucky four. I never saw everyone so eager to work as they were then! More fun!! Today the place is normal once again. The weather is not so good as usual, and everyone is back on the job.

At the present time, I believe Jack and I are going on furlough together on or about March 8. We plan to spend most of it in Scotland. These are just early plans but I hope they work out O.K!

Well, Mom and Dad, there isn't much else to write about today so guess I'll end this letter and head for the showers.

I hope you folks are feeling mighty good and are having a lot of fun!

Everything is O.K. in the United Kingdom.

All my love,

Bob

P.S. A big "Hello" to Art Topp, Oly Olson, and Nappers, for me.

———.

January 20, 1945

Dearest Mom and Dad,

We had a real snowstorm yesterday so it looks like real winter weather. Not very much snow but what there is seems nice.

Mom, you certainly did a wonderful job as installing officer at Eastern Star. Grandma just can't praise you enough. She says you were perfect! And Mom, I know you were!!

I'm very glad that Grandma Packard got to see the apartment before she left for California. I'm sorry that Bud Nordness was discharged. I'm glad he got a good job at Forest Products Lab. He is a good boy! I'm glad you got that nice letter from Jack's mother. Both Jack and Oliver have told me that the pictures reached their homes and wanted me to thank you very much. Jack's dad is a dentist. He is a darn good kid and I know his folks must be mighty nice people! It is swell to hear all the news about everything, Mom and Dad. Thanks a million!!

Gee, Pop, that swell meal you wrote about sounds like a dream! Mom is positively the best cook in the world!! The apartment sounds awfully good to me. I'll bet it looks just about perfect! It will be a big day when I can race up those stairs and surprise you folks! Hope it will be fairly soon! No, Dad, we can't get any films around here. Please say "Hello" to the boys at the office for me.

Keep well, keep happy and have fun! All for now.

All my love,

Bob

.———.

January 22, 1945

Dear Mom and Dad:

I just got a letter from Tom Jones. He is now in Italy and says he is getting along plenty O.K. so far. Here's wishing him all the luck in the world!

Glad all of you are enjoying our new home so much. Everyone writes about how wonderful you have the apartment fixed up, folks. I can hardly wait until I get home again!! The war seems to be going pretty well right now. Let's hope it keeps on that way and ends darn soon. I'm glad Bob K. is stationed in Chicago. It's a wonderful town to be in and will be awfully nice for all concerned to have him so close to home.

Oddie and Frank Larson sent me a swell Xmas card and $1.00; so did Aunt Ruby. Mighty nice of them! Oh yes, I must not forget to mention the nice letter I got from Aunt Ruth! It was a peach!! Everyone is very good to me and I certainly want them to know how much I appreciate it!!

Well Mom and Dad, take it easy, keep well and have fun! I'm feeling plenty O.K. and will write again in a day or so. Enclosed is a little bulletin we received today about the work done by the 8th Air Force in 1944. Thought you might like to have it.

All my love,

Bob

.———.

January 31, 1945

Dear Mom and Dad:

I hope you are feeling real good and have lots of fun. Dad, how is that cold I heard you had? All better I hope! And Mom, how is your back behaving these days? Hope you didn't get too tired in the process of moving. Take good care of yourselves!

I'll have to get busy and write a letter to Kath and Neal pretty soon. Hope they are still enjoying themselves as usual. Gee, but Kath is a wonderful sister. Sure will be happy when you folks and I will be able to drive to Oxford and see her and Neal. Here I am day-dreaming again. Nevertheless I hope my dreams come true before long. Things over here look pretty good these days, don't you agree? We have all kinds of little slogans referring to our return home. Here are a couple or so: "Fort Dix in '46" "Fort Devon in '47," "The Golden Gate in '48 " etc. For myself, I'll take Fort Sheridan as soon as possible!!! More fun, eh! We think of all kinds of crazy things like that everyday, so don't think we will lose our sense of humor. We'll try not to, that's for sure!

Did you know that Phil Gauswitz is engaged? I believe you met his girl, Mom. Her name is Polly. Don't remember her last name, but do know that she is a wonderful girl. They have been going together for over two years, now. She lives in Milwaukee.

Time to get some sleep so will say—good night Mom and Dad.

All my love,

Bob

.———.

WESTERN UNION

CLASS OF SERVICE
This is a full-rate Telegram or Cablegram unless its deferred character is indicated by a suitable symbol above or preceding the address.

1201

SYMBOLS
DL = Day Letter
NL = Night Letter
LC = Deferred Cable
NLT = Cable Night Letter
Ship Radiogram

A. N. WILLIAMS PRESIDENT

The filing time shown in the date line on telegrams and day letters is STANDARD TIME at point of origin. Time of receipt is STANDARD TIME at point of destination

C92 INTL CD SANSORIGINE VIA WUCABLES (5956 31)   1945 FEB 4 PM 3 46

EFM MRS LEN R GAY=

2610 MONROE ST MADISON WIS

=LOVING BIRTHDAY GREETINGS MY THOUGHTS ARE WITH YOU. ALL MY LOVE=

BOB GAY.

WESTERN UNION

CLASS OF SERVICE
This is a full-rate Telegram or Cablegram unless its deferred character is indicated by a suitable symbol above or preceding the address.

1201

SYMBOLS
DL = Day Letter
NL = Night Letter
LC = Deferred Cable
NLT = Cable Night Letter
Ship Radiogram

A. N. WILLIAMS PRESIDENT

The filing time shown in the date line on telegrams and day letters is STANDARD TIME at point of origin. Time of receipt is STANDARD TIME at point of destination

AU22 INTL=CD SANSORIGINE VIA WU CABLES   1945 FEB 17 AM 5 46

EFM MRS LEN R GAY=

2610 MONROE ST MADISON WIS=

LOVE TO MY VALENTINE. ALL MY LOVE=

BOB GAY.

THE COMPANY WILL APPRECIATE SUGGESTIONS FROM ITS PATRONS CONCERNING ITS SERVICE

Bob sent this telegram home for his mom's birthday.

February 9, 1945

Dear Mom and Dad:

The letters have been rolling in the past few days. I now owe fifteen letters to you alone. You can see how much news I've read the past four days! Really swell!! Thanks a million to all!!

Mom and Dad, thanks so much for the interesting clippings, etc. you sent. It was swell to read about the different kids getting married, promoted, etc. Certainly is a neat photo of Colleen Martin! And that snapshot of Carole Rue in Grandma Rue's wedding dress is swell! Carole certainly is a beautiful young lady! Just can't beat these Norwegians!

Well folks, by now you have received letters telling about my Xmas, etc. so I won't repeat all the news about that. I did enjoy opening and getting all the swell gifts I had, very much. Everyone was more than good to me!

Mom, it's plenty O.K. by me if you send pictures to Mrs. Campbell, but we must not let her pay for them. We'll just insist that she shouldn't. Jack has asked to let him pay for them several times, too, but I just tell him that we are happy to do it for them. He says his Mom and Dad are crazy about them and show them to everyone they see. Believe I'll have more snaps to send to you in a few days. Hope these turn out better than the last ones did.

It sure sounds good to hear you speak of my room, my bed, etc. in your letters, folks. My room sounds pretty swell to me! Sure hope I get to see it before many more months go by. Time does go fast over here though. Mom, please don't think that a bit of traffic noise will bother me. I'm quite used to noise during both day and night. Lots of different noises around here all the time. Used to hear plenty of anti-aircraft batteries a few months ago but hardly ever nowadays.

And Mom, your Valentine to me is wonderful. Thank you ever so much! Mom dear, don't worry about me getting into trouble for wearing those plaid socks. Haven't used them as yet cause they look so neat! Just like to see them in with my other stuff. But as for that swell U.W. sweatshirt—well, I wear that plenty! It was sure a great day when it came cause my other heavy shirts were getting washed and it was plenty cold till I put it on! I really love that shirt!

Yes, Mom, I, too, thought about seeing you and Dad off on the train from Chicago on January 14 just a little over a year ago but it seems like it was much longer than that. When we are busy, as we usually are, the days and weeks go by quite fast, but when we think back it seems like much more time has passed than really has. All in all the time has passed quite fast, though! Guess it is cause we lose track of the days, etc. so much by keeping busy.

I have to stop writing now so I can get some chow, so will write another letter, answering more of your good letters, to-night or to-morrow.

Hope you folks are still feeling real well and are having lots of fun. I'm plenty O.K, and all is fine.

All for now,

Your loving son,

Bob

·———·

February 17, 1945

Dear Mom and Pop:

Hi folks I just got back from a two-day pass to London once again. I had quite a good time going to shows, a dance at "Covent Gardens," and eating all the doughnuts I could eat! I stayed at the Hans Crescent Club as I usually do. I rather like this certain Red Cross Club the best because I can easily get to different places from there. When I first get to London I get on the "Underground," or subway as we call it in the States, and head for the Knightsbridge Station. I go to the Red Cross and get my bed, costs 2 shillings (about forty cents) per night. These beds are mostly double-deckers but they do have sheets which really feel good! Anyway I then go out and see the shows, or go to a dance, etc. traveling place to place either by walking or by the Underground if it is quite far. The London Underground is a darn good system. You can really travel fast from place to place. Much better service than by cab or bus. Besides, I still get a kick out of riding the very long escalators. More fun! Usually by the time I get back to the Hans Crescent Club I feel like I was walking on my knees. Sure do a lot of walking in that city.

Oh yes, in a fair-sized city near the base I was looking through a book where fellows sign their names according to states. It was the "State Book" in a little Red Cross Club; anyhow, as I looked over the names from Wisconsin, namely Madison, I saw this name: T/Sgt. Kenneth H. Lindquist, Madison, Wis. 12/31/43. (I believe it said '43 but it may have been '44.) And if I'm not mistaken it is Barbara's brother. His name was the only name I recognized, though.

Dad, I got a big kick out of your letter telling about flowers. You sure are right, Pop! Women really do love flowers!! It was grand to hear all about Mom's swell birthday party. I'm awfully glad everything was so wonderful!

You asked about how we made cocoa in our hut. Well, Mom, we just heat water in our tin cups on the little stove and stir in some cocoa. Sometimes we get a can or so of condensed milk and put some of it in the water, too. We have plenty of cocoa around at present, though.

Oh yes, folks, I managed to get myself a new pair of shoes. They are pretty fair shoes and will last till I get home, I hope! Oh, by the way, Dad, I hope Mr. Williams is over his cold and feeling real good again. Say "Hello" to him for me.

Lots of fun hear about your elevator girls, etc. Pop. I see things are just as interesting as ever! It was good to hear about the horse show in your V-Mail, Mom. Am anxious to get that Air-Mail telling more. Glad Kath did so well!

I'm awfully happy to know that you folks are so well and having fun. Please do keep it up!

I'm feeling fine and all is well in the United Kingdom these days.
Your loving son,
Bob

P.S. Could use a box of candy, cheese, cookies, etc. Please don't go to lots of trouble, though.

Western Union Telegram February 17, 1944
To His Mother

LOVE TO MY VALENTINE. ALL MY LOVE = BOB GAY

•———•

February 18, 1945

Dear mom and dad,

Good morning folks. It is now about seven in the morning and I am at the shop on the flight line. I thought I would type a letter to you on the shop's typewriter while I have a chance so you could see how well these typed V-Mail letters look. I noticed that this ribbon is almost worn out so if this looks a bit light you know why. All of the typed V-Mail I have received from you are very easy to read. The weather today isn't so good so I probably will not have very much work to do. The war news certainly does sound a lot better these days, doesn't it! Hope it won't be long till this mess is over. Did I tell you that I received the last film you sent? Also the inhaler. Thank you very much.

There are a few things I have to do this morning so I guess I had better get started before the best part of the morning is gone. Hope this ribbon isn't too far gone so that it will make this letter faint. Oh yes, the new watch straps are swell. Thank you very much. I will write more tomorrow keep well and have fun... All my love, Bob

•———•

February 22, 1945

Dear Mom and Dad:

I've been keeping pretty darn busy lately, as you can well imagine by the news broadcasts and newspapers. This old war is really going in a big way right now! Maybe it won't last many more months now—sure hope not!

I was working and I broke my good glasses the day before yesterday. I was working on a plane and, as I walked behind the wing as the engines were running, the pilot "revved 'em up" and my glasses just took off and both lenses were smashed to pieces. I didn't do so bad with them though, as this is only the second time I've ever broken them. I have two pair of G.I. glasses though so am getting along O.K. I will send my glasses frame home to you and would appreciate it very much if you would take them to the American Optical Co. and have them all fixed up for me. I'll send the prescription for the lenses along with the glasses. You can probably remember the shape of the lenses—you can always look at a picture of me and see the shape if you are doubtful. There is no terrible hurry about getting them back to me but I do like them an awful lot better than these G.I. ones. So in this package I intend to send in the next few days will be four Air Force pins, my civilian glasses, a few limey postcards, etc. Even the book I promised to send so long age, about Westminster Abbey.

My latest plans for my furlough include a trip to Northern Ireland (probably Belfast) as well as Scotland. Will probably take it during March if I am going to actually take it. If Jack decides not to go I may go by myself. Sure wish I could get home on it, but that is impossible. I feel fine, am getting plenty to eat, etc. All for now as I have to go to work.

Your loving son,
Bob

·———·

March 3, 1945

Dear Mom and Dad:

Gee folks, I sure do owe you a lot of letters! All your letters are swell! They sure make me feel good!

I just got back from a two-day pass to London. Had quite a good time seeing two plays and two movies. Set me back a bit more than I should have spent just preceding my furlough, though. Went with O.K. Larison. Saw George Black's musical comedy, *Strike It Again* and a revue called *Sweeter and Lower*.

Enjoyed them both very much. Also, saw the movies *Practically Yours* with Fred McMurry and Claudette Colbert, and *Meet Me In St. Louis* with Judy Garland and Margaret O 'Brien. They were both excellent! Even had some pretty good ice cream in the Red Cross Club at Rainbow Corner. Sure did taste wonderful!!! Mm mmm!!

Got a very nice letter from Kath today, telling all about the horse show, etc. Also, got a very nice letter from Edith. She seems to like Cornell very much. Glad you had such a nice time celebrating Neal's birthday. It sounds as if Kath is fast becoming a wonderful cook just like you are, Mom! Was sorry to hear about Mrs. Worth breaking her wrists. Hope she will soon be O.K!

Oh yes, I got the box of cookies from Grandma Lee, Mom. They sure were delicious! And Mom dear, you pack the boxes mighty fine as they always come through in perfect shape. Thanks very much!

Boy oh boy, I'll bet Pop's new outfit is really neat! Looks like Speth's have some good snappy clothes. Good boy, Pop!

Bet you look *SWELL*!!

Dad, I'm sure glad you don't have walks to shovel, ashes to carry out, and lawns to mow this year. It will be kinda nice for you and Mom to get a little rest from that sort of thing for a change.

Mom, glad you got another ribbon for your good service at the U.S.O. You sure do your full share, Mom dear. Mom dear. You are a peach!!!

Pop, you really have done a great job on the oil board & sure sounds like a fine record, and I know how hard you have worked on it. Maybe they will make you an oil coordinator pretty soon, eh? Hope so, cause you would do a darn good job! Glad to hear the NEW apartments are full. Hope they keep that way, Pop. Oh yeah, I enjoyed the joke about the deer a lot! Pretty neat!!

Well folks, guess I'd better get some sleep. Keep well and have fun.

Could use some finger nail scissors, some more good cookies, and a candy bar or so, if you can get them.

Your loving son,

Bob

•————•

March 8, 1945

Dearest Mom and Dad:

It was nice to hear your stories about the U.S.O. Yes, Mom, I know what you mean when you say, "There are all kinds and types of guys in this old Army." Was also very interesting to hear about Truax. I'm sure happy that you folks have kept so well this past year. I, too, have been very well. Let's all try our best to stay that way! I enjoyed hearing about Kath, Yippee and the kitten. They certainly do have a great time, don't they!

Glad you heard from Stuart in the Philippines. Evidently he is O.K. as he is such a nice guy. Please give him a big "Hello" from me when you next write him, Mom. Glad he sent that Jap note for our book, Mom. Gee, the books must be getting quite large by now, eh?

I'm fine and all is going very well now. Since I last wrote my furlough was cancelled, but is now open again so I really do believe I'll get off on it approx. the 18th of this month as I have written before. Guess I'll be going by myself, but am going nevertheless!

Weather here has been quite good lately. Take good care of yourselves and have fun!!!

All my love,
Bob.

P.S. Thanks so much for the nice birthday kiss, Mom. Will collect it when I get home!
P.S.S. Enclosed is 14 snapshots and 14 negatives.

[Written by censor:]
4 SNAPSHOTS AND 4 NEGATIVES REMOVED BECAUSE THEY VIOLATE CENSORSHIP REGULATIONS.

•————•

March 13, 1945

Dear Mom and Dad:

Gee, we sure have had some swell weather today! Didn't even need a jacket until six p.m. And, Dad, THANKS A MILLION for sending me that money order. Had it cashed today and am all set to leave on furlough March 18 as planned. It sure was wonderful of you to send so much. THANKS AGAIN, DAD!!

Was in London the other day, and while listening to the good old juke box in the Red Cross I saw an old friend I used to know at Kearns, Utah last year. Perhaps you remember my writing about him. He is John Copeland of Findley, Ohio. Really a swell guy! He is a radio operator… [Rest of the page was cut out by censor.]

I spent about two hours with him and really had a very interesting time listening to his story. He said the Swedes really treated them swell and that they are about the finest and cleanest people he has ever seen. Said the country is wonderful, cities are new and very modern, girls are blond, clean, and very pretty. Anyway, he just couldn't say enough for them. Would like to tell you more about his experiences but it will have to wait till I get home.

Take it easy and have fun, Mom and Dad!

Your loving son,

Bob

.———.

Western Union Telegram
March 16, 1944

THANKS FOR MONEY RECEIVED FONDEST GREETINGS = BOB GAY

.———.

AUTHOR'S NOTE

Bob had a seven-day furlough and used it to spend days in Belfast, Northern Ireland. He fell in love with the people and countryside. He would talk about them for the rest of his life.

.————.

March 27, 1945

Dear Mom and Dad:

I just got back from Ireland last night and I want you to know right away that I had a wonderful time!!!! I feel swell, had perfect weather, and met a wonderful little girl!

Guess I'll start from the beginning if I can come down enough to write so you will be able to make it out.

I left here around noon on the 17th, arrived in London later the same day, went to a good movie and spent the night in the Red Cross at Knightsbridge Station in London. Couldn't get my train out of London till 4:50 p.m. so just spent the day walking around and eating donuts, ice cream, and cookies in the Red Cross at Rainbow Corner in Piccadilly.

Left London at 4:50 p.m. and arrived in Stranraer, Scotland about 4:15 a.m. Got aboard ship and after seeing the third-class section, I and another G.I. decided to transfer to first class and get a cabin. We did so for about six shillings or $1.20 and some welcome sleep. Boat left about 8:30 a.m. and I got into Larne, North Ireland around 10:30 or 11:00 a.m., jumped on a train and was in Belfast by noon.

Went to the Red Cross, which is the best one I have yet seen, checked my bag, got a bed and went out to see the town.

It is a wonderful place and more like home than any place I've yet seen over here. Very much like Americans in dress, talk (what I mean is in their friendliness, etc. as they do have a real brogue, believe me) and so on. They love the Americans and I believe the feeling is about mutual in that respect. They are a proud people, love to talk with us, and can't seem to do enough for us.

When I left here I intended to stay in Belfast 3 days then go to Scotland, but after seeing the place, and thinking over what I had heard about Scotland I decided to spend all my time in Belfast and its vicinity. Honestly, Mom and Dad, I had a wonderful time! I can't say enough for those people and their country.

I met a very, very nice girl who is from Erie, South Ireland and works in Belfast. Southern Ireland is neutral so we cannot go there, as we would be interned, but the Irish can travel back and forth from north to south freely. She has the cutest brogue and boy oh boy is she pretty! Anyway, I had five days of beautiful weather and a most perfect time.

I went to some dog races and it was a lot of fun; made a few bets, won some and lost some—came out about even financially, so all was swell. Another fellow, named Paul Rhylander from Providence Rhode Island and I went on a swell bicycle ride all over the place. Went to Bellevue Park, a very swell place.

The beds in the Red Cross were fine and we had lots and lots of delicious fresh eggs every day there. Had a lot of milk and even a few steaks! Boy oh boy, was that milk ever good!

I went to some dances, etc. Gosh folks, I had a swell time!! My morale is up to a new high right now! I have a lot of wonderful memories to keep forever, and to hide many unpleasant things that we often witness whether we want to or not.

I had to be back here by midnight yesterday. Wouldn't have left Belfast until Sunday if there would have been a boat coming over, but there are no ceilings on Sunday so left Saturday night and got in London on about noon. Stayed overnight and came back to the base on Monday.

I have many nice cards, booklets, etc. to send home to you. Also have some really nice genuine Irish linen handkerchiefs. Some for you, Mom, and you, Pop, and Kath too. And Mom, if you would like to give one of them to Grandma Gay, Grandma M, etc. it is O.K. by me. The ones for Kath could be sort of a birthday present for her. They are really fine hankies as you will see.

I must get busy now so will say good night for now and will write again tomorrow. Have many fine letters to answer, etc. I'm very happy, and a very lucky guy! Take good care of yourselves.

All my love,

Bob

·———·

March 29, 1945

Dear Mom and Dad,

I sent an Air-Mail to you yesterday and I hope it reaches you quite soon. I told you all about my swell furlough. Guess I didn't tell you that my transportation both ways was paid for by Uncle Sam Starting just a few days before my furlough began, you as soldiers started to get travel warrants giving free transportation on furloughs, and now also for 48-hour passes. Pretty nice of course it saves a few pounds for us to spend elsewhere.

I've received several very nice birthday cards besides those two nice packages you sent. Thanks a million folks. I hope to see you before my next birthday. At least on a furlough!! Gee, here I am 22 years old and I don't feel any older than I did yesterday!! Think of that!!!

I feel swell and all is going along in grand style!

All my love,

Bob

·———·

April 2, 1945

Dear Mom and Dad:

I want to thank you folks again for my wonderful birthday presents, the $50 and packages. You're wonderful, Mom and Pop!! Mom I'm glad you are feeling so awfully good!!! Keep it up, and don't worry about getting on a few extra pounds!!

Dad, thanks for the news about the Martins, Russ Slightum, etc. Always like to hear about the uptown goings-on! Glad to hear that Jack McCann's wife is so nice, Mom. Think I'll be able to do so well for myself sometime? Hope so!!!

Mom, congratulations on your award for 200 hours at the U.S.O.!!!

Mom, in one V-Mail to me you asked if I minded the sea. No, Mom, I don't mind it at all. In fact, I rather like it. And, Mom,

I've never yet been seasick, and even the mildest form. I've sure seen a lot of people get seasick, though. Guess I'm just lucky once again! I think the reason most people get seasick is because they think about it all the time and don't eat enough. I never miss a meal on a ship, but never think about getting seasick, and spend a lot of time on deck in the fresh air. Really is a lot of fun, although it gets boring at times.

Mom, you asked if I ever see the Norske Marine gal—no, Mom, she has moved on somewhere, darn it! But I do go out with an A.T.S. girl (British W.A.C.) now and then. She is a nice kid but I couldn't get serious about her.

Mom, guess what! Yesterday I got a package from you that was mailed on September 12, 1944. It was a box of candy from the chocolate shop, some candy bars, and some peanuts. Always in good shape except the peanuts were stale. Candy was O.K. and enjoyed by us all. Thanks a lot!

I hope to fly to Belfast on a two-day pass sometime between now and June 1. It sure is a swell place!!

I have some nice things from Ireland to send to you. We'll fix up a box and get it on the way in a day or two!

Glad to know Bob Fisher is alive. He shouldn't be a prisoner very much longer now.

Dad, thanks for the nice pin-up you enclosed in Mom's letter of March 21. Sure would like a cutie like that to wake me up instead of one of these characters here.

Keep well and have fun!

All my love, Bob

·———·

Western Union Telegram
April 13, 1945

DEAR DAD A BIG HAPPY BIRTHDAY TO YOU LOVE = BOB GAY.

·———·

April 14, 1945

Dear Mom and Dad:

In the past few days many important events have happened to affect the whole world. That's for sure!

I certainly am very sorry that President Roosevelt died during what is probably the most important time in his, and for that matter in all of our lives. Even though I didn't agree with all of his policies, I know that he was truly a very great man!! The whole world has lost a lot, especially the people of America, in the deaths of President Roosevelt and Wendel Willkie.

The war news certainly is good these days, though. I don't believe it will last much longer over here. The sooner the crazy Germans quit, the sooner we can all be together again. Probably will have to make another stop or so before a lot of us get home—well, time will tell!!

I've three swell V-Mails from you, Mom dear. Latest one is of April 5!! It sure is wonderful to hear about Kath and Neal, Grandma Gay, Ed and Connie, etc. Sorry to hear of the death of Phil Baldwin. Sure will be a lot of wonderful guys missing after this mess is over. I hope Dr. Fauerbach hears that Bob is O.K. real soon!!

Take good care of yourselves and say "Hello" to all for me.

Your loving son,

Bob

———

April 21, 1945

Dear Mom and Dad,

Sorry I've not written for the past few days but I've had no time of my own. I just now finished 5 days of K.P.—you see, all winter they had permanent K.P.s, but now all staff sergeants and below pull it for 5 days at a time. I won't get it again now for quite a long time - at least I shouldn't!! 3:00 a.m. till 7:00 p.m. straight. Really feel like going to bed when a day of K.P. is over!

April 15, 1945

Dear Bob,

Everything is going as usual. Madison doesn't look any different this spring than it did last year and the year before. The plumb and apple trees are in bloom now and the cherry trees have been blooming for over a week. The lilacs are just starting to blossom - they are 2 or 3 weeks earlier than usual. I have been working in the arboretum afternoons and consequently have had a chance to watch all the buds come in.

The latest news is that Gussy just made Phi Beta Kappa. He now belongs to 3 honory fraternities, 1 social and 1 professional fraternity - that is our man.

Your furlough sounded very interesting. I sure would like to see some of that country. I guess if I hadn't gotten the ax I would have been seeing quite a bit of northern Italy with Tom. I stopped in to see Mr. & Mrs. Jones on the way the Sig Phi house last Sunday

were listening to the army hour. They mentioned the last time you were in to see them and they (with everybody else) said how glad they would be to see you again soon. They worry a lot about Tom so I guess he has really hit some tough going.

I see Juicy - old Juicy - every now and then - he certainly has changed. You wouldn't know.

I want to drop a note to Lee and Tom yet tonite so I'll close now.

Take it easy, Bob.

Asyeuer,

Pepper -

Letter from Pepper (Arnold) Jackson, who started the Jackson Clinic in Madison, Wisconsin.

Anyway, tomorrow I'm going on a tour possibly a 3-day pass so won't be able to write till I return from it.

I'm really a pretty tired kid tonight so we'll say good night Mom and Dad. Keep well and have fun.

Your loving son, Bob

•————•

April 26, 1945

Dear Mom and Dad:

I just returned from a three-day pass and found several wonderful letters from you, Kath, the Sasmans, Phil Gauswitz, Jackie, etc. I am never very happy about coming back to camp after pass, but when I find such swell letters it gives me a wonderful feeling that brightens up everything!

Mom, you write me so many swell letters and always apologize when you miss a day or so. Really, *Mom dear, you are so wonderful*!!! *Thanks Mom* more than I can ever express in mere words!!

I had quite nice weather on this pass, really had a fine time. I walked all over Hyde Park the other afternoon. It really was beautiful! All the nice trees and grass, and people paddling about on the little lake (the Serpentine). I met a very cute little girl. She is a nurse in the Royal Cancer Hospital in London, near Hyde Park. We had a lot of fun together. Went walking, and to a movie (*A Tree Grows in Brooklyn*), and then to a dance. She had to be in by midnight though, Mom, so you can see I got my beauty sleep O.K. Her name is Jean Maguire. She isn't very tall, has the prettiest blue eyes, and her hair is about the same as Kath's. Really a cute little girl!

I have met quite a few people from many different places, as you said Mom; and to be honest with you I must say that as a whole, the Irish are the nicest and most friendly. Only wish I could meet some more Norskys, especially a little Norsky girl!

It was really swell to hear about your fine time at the Gay Houslet Ranch!! Seriously Mom, I'm awfully glad you had so much fun. Your letters tell so much I can just about imagine that I have been there!

Guess I won't get to fly to Belfast after all. We did have a plane going there from our base every two days but about three days ago the service was discontinued. Oh well, I saw it once!

Enjoyed the clipping about Truax very much. Would I ever like to be one of those overseas veterans to work on the line there! Glad Uncle John and Aunt Maude were over to see you. Hope they were fine and enjoyed their Florida trip very much. Also were glad that you were at Aunt Maude's for Pop's birthday. Bet you had a fine time, eh Pop? So little Jonnie Wileden liked those pants as much as ever! Glad he has them, Mom. Oh yes, Mom, please don't send any more films till I request them again. Have several on hand now and when my stock gets low I'll request some as you asked me to do. Sorry Don Oscar is in the hospital again. Hope he will be O.K. real soon! Mom, I hope you didn't get too tired washing the wall in the hallway. You shouldn't do it!! And, Mom, Jack Campbell is O.K. and we are just as good pals as ever!! His mom has been in the hospital in San Francisco for about five weeks but she is home and all O.K. once again, so Jack tells me. All of us are well and getting on as well as usual.

Today we got shots once again, had another typhoid and cholera shot plus a new small pox vaccination. Also had all of our records checked. Oh yes, we had some ice cream in the mess hall this noon! First time we ever had any on the base. We can get a bit of it in the Red Cross Club at Rainbow at the Rainbow Corner in London, though. Sure did taste good!! Also had fresh eggs (cold storage, but fried and not powdered) for a change!

I usually go on pass by myself cause I find that I have just as good a time alone as with someone, never have to argue about where to go and what to do, etc.

Well, Mom and Pop, guess I better go to bed now so will say good night, keep well and have fun!!

Your loving son,

Bob

P.S. let's hope my next stop will be in the U.S.A., at least long enough for a furlough to see you! Time will tell.

.———.

April 29, 1945

Dear Mom and Pop,

Surprise we had this morning when we got up: the ground was covered with about 2 in. of snow, and it was still snowing! Now it has almost all melted, the sun is out, and it is warmer than it has been for the past few days. We never expected snow after the wonderful weather we had the first 3 weeks of this month.

Well, today was payday and I got my usual number of pounds, shillings, etc. and am anxious to go on a pass once again.

Tell Grandma M. that the little Irish girl in Belfast did not have red hair. There are a lot of redheads here in England but many in Ireland.

We were all very sorry to find out of the death of Ernie Pyle. He was a wonderful man all right!

Yes Mom, April 21 was our big anniversary just as you mentioned. It was just another day though.

Dad, you sure have an impressive list of elevator operators. Enjoyed seeing the list and also your bit of poetry. My package containing my glasses, etc. any day now. Keep well and have fun—

All my love,
Bob

· ———— ·

May 1, 1945

Dear Mom and Dad,

Mom, it was fun hearing about your big day when Aunt Oly, Grandma Lee, Oddie, and Bob Sasman all paid you a visit. I know Bob's commission would not change him a bit. He is the same swell guy he has always been!

Dad, I'm sure glad you received my cable on your birthday! Very happy you had such a wonderful party at Aunt Maude's. Sure wish I could have been there. Glad to know that the old electric razor has appeared again! Tell Kath to keep in practice baking those swell pies I hear so much about. I hope to taste one in the not-too-distant future.

Love Bob

P.S. What is our new telephone number? Might want it in a hurry someday. Never can tell!

.————.

May 6, 1945

Dear Mom and Dad,

I just returned from a short pass to London. Went down to see the little nurse I mentioned a while back. We went out for dinner and to a movie called *Here Come the Co-Eds* with Abbot and Costello. It was a good show and we had a swell time.

I got your V-Mails of April 26 and 28 today Mom. They were swell!!

I doubt if I'll ever get back to Belfast cause they discontinued the plane trips I told you about. Well, anyway, I saw it once so guess I can't complain. Yes, Mom, I did get a very nice Xmas card from Aunt Patton—I believe I told you before. Hope your cold is better Pop!

Lots of good news in the papers lately, eh!!

Loads of love,

Bob

.————.

May 8, 1945

Dear Mom and Dad,

Isn't this a wonderful day!!!! Boy oh boy!! Two down and one to go. Last night the sky around here was lit up with colored flares. We could see them going up from our field and fields way off in the distance. Sure was a pretty sight.

We were restricted to the base as of noon yesterday. Hope we will be allowed out again in a day or so. The lucky guys who happened to be on pass got them automatically extended for 48 hours. Wish it could have happened to me. Anyway, we all have a most wonderful feeling to know it is over on this side.

For the last couple of weeks the group has been hauling food to Holland. Now I don't know what is next. We won't be very busy now that the war in Europe is over so are all anxious to get on the move again. Don't know where we will go from here for sure but hope it will be home for a furlough. Things look fairly good in that prospect.

The English have declared today and tomorrow a national holiday, and there is a lot of celebrating in every city and town.

The weather has warmed up, the sun is shining, etc. All in all everything is WONDERFUL!!

Keep well, keep happy, and have fun!!

Your loving son,

Bob

P.S. No need to send any more packages unless I especially request them. All is O.K!!!

•————•

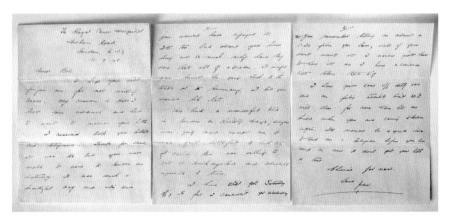

Letter from a gal Bob met on April 26, 1945, who worked at the London Royal Cancer Hospital as a nurse.

May 11, 1945

Dear Mom and Dad,

We now are allowed one (1) three-day pass per month and that is all. We all have Sunday off but can only get a short pass from 9 a.m. to 12 p.m. It is supposed to be a day of rest. Therefore, I can only get to London once a month—too bad cause I've got a pretty swell girlfriend down there.

Also they now blow the old bugle morning and night so it is almost like we used to have it in the States.

We are plenty busy again though we aren't carrying bombs anymore. This place is full of rumors, some good—others not so hot. Time will tell!!

All for now—

Love, Bob

Western Union Telegram
May 14, 1945

MY LOVE AND GREETINGS ON MOTHERS DAY.

YOU ARE MORE THAN EVER IN MY THOUGHTS AT THIS TIME. BEST WISHES AND GOOD HEALTH = BOB GAY.

May 16, 1945

Dear Mom and Dad:

So far we are still at the same old base and although there are lots of good ol' rumors around I believe we will be here for a while yet. Never can tell when or where it will be next, but I'm sure hoping that I'll get home for a furlough before we get near the country of "Yellow Men." Time will tell.

I'm glad you all liked the shamrock seeds, hankies, etc. Only wish I could have gotten some more nice things. There was one beautiful table set in particular that I knew you would be crazy

Irish linen hankies and shamrock seeds Bob sent his mom from Belfast.

about, Mom. It was really a beautiful piece of linen, cost approx. 15 pounds so I couldn't quite make it. Anyway, I had a marvelous time when I was there, and knowing that you did like what I did send home makes everything perfect! Glad Grandpa M. took some of those shamrock seeds. Hope they grow O.K. The picture of the boat wasn't the actual one I went on from Scotland to Ireland, but it is quite similar.

Bet the capital really looks neat all lit up once again. It certainly is wonderful here just seeing lights in windows again. Oh yes, Mom, thanks for sending Kath's letter to you of April 26. I got a big kick out of it. She and Neal certainly do have a lot of fine times together! I'm sure glad they are so happy. I have three letters from her to answer today. I'm afraid Kath's friend, Emily, made a big mistake marrying Eddie B. Never know.

Yes, Mom and Dad, it is over, over here. We are mighty glad about it, but always have in our minds the thought that the Japs are still left.

Also, thanks for the clippings, newspaper pages, *Wisconsin News Digest*, etc. you have sent me from time to time. I got a letter from Stanley Clemens, Pepper and Phil last week. Haven't heard from Tom for some time now, hope he is O.K. Phill and Polly said I must have dinner with them as soon as possible after they are married. They don't intend to be married for a while, though, because Phil must finish medical school first. At least that is the present plans, I guess. SWELL PAIR!!

I hope you are well and having as much fun as always. I'm fine and all is O.K!

All my love,

Bob

.————.

Mendlesham, England
May 21, 1945

Dear Mom and Dad:

Well folks, at long last they have lifted the censorship on certain subjects so I can now tell you how I came over, etc.

When I last talked to you on the phone, Easter Sunday, April 9, 1944, I was at Camp Myles Standish, Mass. My last pass in the good old U.S.A. was a twelve-hour pass to Providence, R.I.

On April 12th we boarded a huge troop train at Myles Standish. We were loaded with packs, carbines, ammunition, knives, gas masks, steel helmets, etc. Really looked like a rough bunch of characters.

After a short train ride we pulled up on the docks in Boston, and there was our ship, the U.S.S. *Wakefield*. This ship was formerly the luxury liner *Manhattan*, which was bombed at Singapore, run aground some place or other. However, it had been turned into an excellent troop ship. Everything was steel so as to be fire proof, etc., and this was her maiden voyage as a troop ship. We boarded ship on the 12th with thousands of other troops. They laded ship all of the afternoon and most of the night. We started out at 4 a.m. on the 13th of April.

The U.S.S. *Wakefield* is a large fast boat. This trip was her first one as a troop ship. We did not go by convoy, as we had a fast, well-armed ship. We enjoyed watching the sailors and marines have gunnery practice most every day.

We were really packed in! The bunks were five high and so close together that two men had to squeeze to pass between the tiers. The space between you and the guy about was about two feet so if you were on the bunk you had to lie down.

I spend most of every day on deck. I really would have enjoyed the trip if only we could have had some good food. We were fed twice a day, mostly dehydrated food which is sad stuff!! Anyway, I didn't get sick at all—and sure am mighty glad of it!!! There were an awful lot of guys sick, and they sure were miserable fellows!

We zig-zagged all over the ocean, went close to the coast of Iceland, and up north of Ireland, then came down between Ireland and Scotland to Liverpool. Here we disembarked on April 21. A trip of nine days. It took a long time to unload. When I got off it was about 2 a.m. of the 22nd. We marched for about two miles or so to a train station. It was the blackest night I've ever seen my life! It was so dark that it was actually impossible to see the guy in front of you. And did the packs ever get heavy. Wow!!

We got a queer little English train (queer looking then, but quite a common sight now) and moved on. The sun came out at dawn and as it was spring the little fields, lined with hedges, looked wonderful after that water.

Our trip over wasn't especially eventful, although we did have quite a bit of rough weather and the old baby really rolled. Was kind of fun except for the poor fellows that were sick. Good many were plenty sick on our worst night when things were really bouncing about.

We arrive at this very base at noon on the 22nd of April, and we are still here in the same old hut. This is the Mendlesham Airdrome about a mile from Mendlesham, about 12 miles from Ipswich on the road from Ipswich to Norwich. We are in the Suffolk country. It's about 92 miles to London from the base.

After I get to Ipswich from the base, I can get to London in about two hours. Pretty nice to have a large place to go to on pass. Have only one three-day pass per month, now. Don't especially like Ipswich so generally go to London.

Well, Mom and Dad, got to tell you something of interest for a change, didn't I? Wish I had as much to write about every day!

Yesterday I got three letters, and Air-Mail of May 7, from you, Mom; a V-Mail from both of you written on the 10th, and another V-Mail from Mom of the 11th. All were wonderful, Mom and Pop. Thanks a million!!!!

Ed's new Chris Craft sure sounds swell!! Hope he'll give me a ride in it some time. He sure does have a lot of fun, doesn't he! Oh yes, thanks for the clippings, Mom, and also for those new papers you get at the drug store. Glad you folks had such a nice time at Aunt Ruby's. Hope they are fine over there. It was awfully nice of you to send one of those hankies to Grandma Lee for Mother's Day, Mom. Thanks very much!!! And Mom the same goes for the nice little gift to Grandma Gay. You are such a wonderful Mom!!!

You mentioned something about the points for demobilization. Well folks, I have 61 points so am still standing short. We do not get any points for the Unit Citation, and so far haven't received any cluster to put on it. My points are as follows:

28 months service ....28 points
13 months overseas..13 points
4 battle stars (5 points each...........................<u>20 points</u>
Total   61 points

Pops, glad your elevators are still full of operators. Pretty good way to put it don't you think? Good to hear that the Plymouth is still going good, and that everything uptown is too. Say "Hell" to the boys for me.

Yes, Mom, I still remember the old phone numbers: Home F.3963, office B.2765, Sasmans B.3317, etc. Sure am glad we have the same good old number. Hope I get to use it sometime this summer! Don't know where the next stop will be, but guess it doesn't hurt to hope. Only time will tell where we go from here.

Keep well, keep happy, and have fun!

Lots of love,

Bob

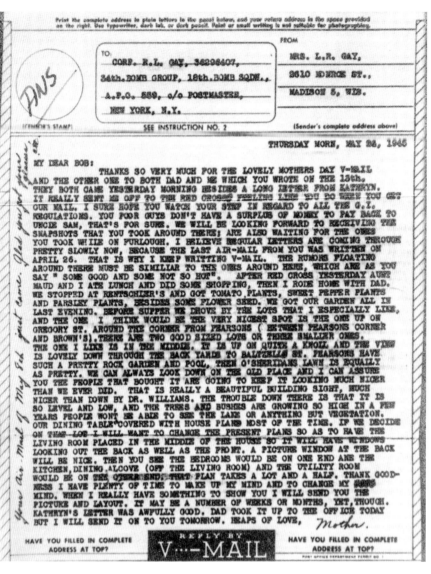

V-Mail from home.

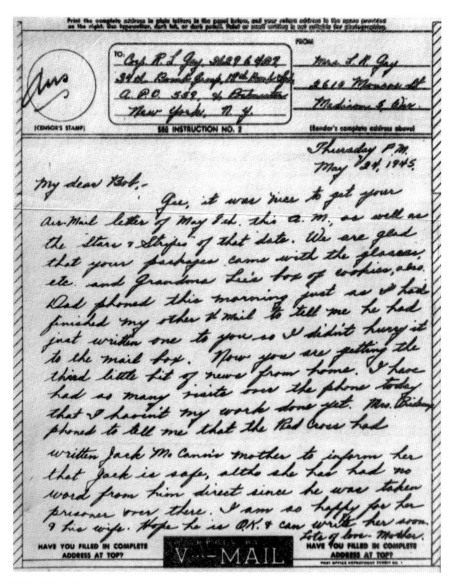

V-Mail from home.

·———·

May 25, 1945

Dear Mom and Dad:

This country has weather changes so often and at such unconceivable times that it isn't possible to plan on the sun coming out tomorrow. One day it is almost hot and on the next one we can use a fire. Strange place, even after my year plus a month or so. Oh well, won't worry about that!!

You mentioned the tour over Germany that was being given to some ground crew personnel. Well Mom, none of us got to go on them. They were all ready to take one bunch over a few weeks ago but the trip was scrubbed because of bad weather. Never have taken any from here and doubt if they will do so now. Some fellows from other groups got to go, though. It would have been a nice trip.

I'm glad you received the cable for Mother's Day O.K., Mom dear. Only wish it would have come to you on Sunday morning as I had planned!!

So my Mom and Pop are getting a bit chubby!! I think it's wonderful! Can hardly wait to see how you look! Of course I know why you are putting on a few pounds—it's because of your cooking, Mom, and Olson's swell bakery so close. Just as you said, Pop!! Glad you have had so much fun going to horse sales with Kath and Neal, etc. I'm glad you got to see the air show at Truax. I'll bet it was interesting for you to see. Hope Jack passed his algebra exam O.K. With you to give him help, I know he must have made it. He sure has my sincerest sympathy. I'd hate to face a big algebra test. It would scare me quite a bit!!

May 29, 1945

Hello again. I just got back from my three-day pass and will now finish this letter I started on the 25th. I can't take another pass now till the 22nd of next month—that is, if we are still here.

I had a very nice time. Stayed in the Red Cross on Saturday night, then thought I'd try to get a room at the Regent Palace Hotel as it was near the end of the month and not as crowded as usual. Anyway, I was lucky and got a nice room. Slept on a beautiful thick mattress. Boy, ho I did sleep!!! Sunday a.m. I walked about in Hyde Park and also Green Park. It was a very fine morning. Listened to the different characters giving their speeches at Marble Arch. What a sight to see! Went out with Jean on each of the three evenings I was there. She had to work till 8 p.m. all three of the days so we usually just went out to some restaurant, had a bit to eat and then would go for a walk. She certainly is a very nice girl. I know you would like her. Don't worry about me getting married or anything like that though. I'm still all for the American girls!!! However, she certainly is a wonderful little gal and has helped me to keep a happy outlook on everything. A great morale builder.

I got a nice letter from Jo the other day. She is now managing a photography studios, like the one in Manchester's, at Allentown, Penn. She is only a couple of hours from New York City and told me to call her up if I should happen by one of these days. She sure has done O.K. for herself, hasn't she!

Also got some clippings from your folks, a letter from you, Mom, one from Gene and another from Hazel Rue. Thanks a million!! All were swell!!!!

I'm feeling swell, and if all goes as it appears to be I'll be even happier before long.

I hope the weather at home is now as it should be in May. Keep well and have fun!!

All my love,
Bob

·———·

June 3, 1945

Dear Mom and Dad:

Hope you are enjoying some nice sunny, summer weather these days. Received your V-Mail of May 21 yesterday, Mom. Thanks a million! Glad you are having as much fun as always with the Prideauxs, Ed and Connie, etc. say "Hello" to them for me.

Mom, I see you are keeping plenty busy. *Please* don't work too hard!!!

Pop, I'd sure like to see that tie Uncle Sid and Uncle John got you in Chicago. Bet it's a honey!! How about me borrowing it one of these days?

Kath sure is having a wonderful time! I'm mighty glad she married Neal. They love the life they are leading almost beyond description. Kath writes me very nice little letters, and quite often, too! I've certainly got a wonderful little sister!!! She always tells me about every visit you folks make, and certainly does love it when you come to see them.

Well, Mom and Dad, nothing new to write about. All the news about my next move sounds *very* good. I only hope it turns out that way. Keep well and have fun!!!

Lots of love,
Bob.

·———·

June 5, 1945

Dear Mom and Dad:

Received V-Mail letters from each of you. Good to hear that all is so well in the good old home town.

So far I haven't been fined for anything. Now that we are in the bait of saluting again, etc., it really isn't bad at all. Pop, glad to hear that Doc Donkle was in to see you. Sounds as if Navy life is agreeing with him quite well!! Glad to hear that Harry Stoll is getting along so well. Same goes for Don Williams. Nice to hear the gasoline rations are being increased. Hope the Plymouth will keep going till new cars are plentiful again. Glad you folks have the "last 40" plowed. Hope to get a look at that garden this summer!

Gee, I sure have my fingers crossed for Neal. Hope he gets the priority for that truck O.K. It's a lot of fun to hear about the house plans, lots, etc. Everything sounds swell!!! The lot near the Pearsons is plenty nice. Swell neighbors and everything.

Mighty glad to hear that Jack McCann is O.K! Hope he will get home soon!!

Weather today is cool and cloudy, but the rumors are bright and hot!!! Wow!! They are taking our blouses away and are replacing them with short jackets made of material somewhat like that of the blouses, but not quite as good.

Please give Aunt Maude and Uncle John a special "Hello" from me. In fact, a big hello to the whole family would be in order! We aren't very busy these days and the sooner we move the better. Believe me, Mom and Dad, everything is shaping up *very*, *very*, good over here. We are all feeling very happy these days.

Sure will have a lot of nice pin-up girls here when we leave, but we'll donate them, very gladly, to the Limies [*sic*].

Keep well and have fun!!

Lots of love,

Bob

•————•

June 16, 1945

Dear Mom and Dad:

Hope there is lot of good fresh milk to be had, cause YOUR BOY IS COMING HOME!!

I'm sure a happy guy these days. If I had left here are originally planned I would have probably been home by now. The suspense of waiting kinda gets on our nerves—and it still seems like a dream. Just can't seem to realize that we are really coming home!!!! I can hardly wait!!! You know, I've a good possibility of being home, or at least in the States before you get this letter. I sure hope I'll beat it home. We'll see!!

Haven't written since June 5 and will explain when I see you. Thought we would be on our way before now.

Your swell letters are still rolling in. Thanks a million!!!

PLEASE KEEP WELL AND GIVE MY LOVE TO ALL!!! So long for now,

All my love,

Bob

P.S. I'm fine—and very happy!!!

·———·

NOTE FROM MOM

Bob returned home on B-17 Ship #326.

June 17, 1945: Took off from Mendlesham Airdrome, England at 0600. Landed at Valley, Wales at 0730. Flight time 1 hour and 30 minutes.

June 18, 1945: Took off from Valley, Wales at 0855. Landed on Terceira Island in the Azores, on Lugen Field at 1819. (Time now moved 2 hours back.) Flight time 9 hours and 24 minutes, all over water.

June 19–21, 1945: Stayed in Azores due to weather conditions.

June 22, 1945: Took off at 0850 for Gander, Newfoundland. Landed at 1840. Flight time 9 hours and 50 minutes. All over water.

June 23, 1945: Took off from Gander, Newfoundland at 1200. Landed at Bradley Field, Connecticut at 1830. Flight time 6 hours and 30 minutes.

·———·

Western Union Telegram
June 23, 1945

DEAR FOLKS ARRIVED IN CONN BY PLANE FEEL SWELL SEE YOU IN A FEW DAYS 30 DAY FURLOUGH LOVE = BOB

·———·

NOTE FROM MOM

Bob phoned from Camp Myles Standish, Mass. on Monday morning, June 25, at 7:15 o'clock.

AUTHOR'S NOTE

Bob would go to Fort Snelling, Minnesota, where he would spend a few days before the official furlough. After that furlough, he had orders to report to Sioux Falls, South Dakota.

CHAPTER 13

SIOUX FALLS, SOUTH DAKOTA

Sioux Falls Army Air Field, Sioux Falls, South Dakota
August 7, 1945

Dear Mom and Dad:

We arrived here at 8:00 a.m. yesterday as expected. So far we have done nothing. We are waiting to be processed and should get going on that in the next day or so.

Here we are put into one of four classes. Class 1 goes overseas right away, class 2 trains a while and then is eligible to go overseas, class 3W will get permanent party jobs on bases in the States, and class 4 will be eligible for discharge. I will, almost without a doubt get in a class 3W and get a permanent party job in the States. Pretty darn swell! Also get those two other Battle Stars—71 points total.

Jack Campbell got here yesterday afternoon and is here in the service club with me now. He is almost sure to get into class 3W also in fact all of us ground personnel who were overseas before December 1, 1944, will stay in the States. We will not stay in the 34th Bomb Group anymore but as soon as I have processed and know what class I'm in for sure I will phone and tell you.

I've seen lots of the old gang here but understand that some of the boys still in England may still be there until sometime in November.

Keep well and have fun!

All my love, Bob

•————·

Western Union Telegram
August 7, 1945

DEAR FOLKS AM GETTING BETTER DEAL THAN EXPECTED MORE
NEWS LATER WILL CALL THE NEXT FEW DAYS ALL MY LOVE = BOB

•————·

August 16, 1945

Dear Mom and Dad:

Here I am still sitting around waiting for my orders. Tomorrow some of us will be on K.P. to help some of the time away. Everyone pulls it here, master sergeants on down, so can't complain a bit by this time.

Guys are shipping out fast now so hope to go darn soon. So far only received one letter since I last phoned. It was from Pepper. I think they are putting my mail in with the Grays instead of Gays. Anyway I'll get the other sooner or later.

Jack Campbell left for Colorado Springs, Colorado yesterday. Fernandes and Glenn are still here. Is Dick Levnick home yet? Heard over the radio that the 31st bomber group docked last Saturday. I hear from Tom Jones he is home. Hope he drops in to see you soon.

I've got lots of new clothes, shoes, etc. Plenty of money, too.

Glad gasoline is off the ration list. Pretty nice to know you can get plenty of gas, eh Pop? Guess I rather cut your coupons down while I was home.

All for now,
Love Bob

SURE IS GREAT TO HAVE THIS WAR OVER. NOW WE JUST SWEAT OUT OUR GRADUATION PAPERS.
Please excuse my messy writing as I'm writing on my bed—rather awkward.

.————.

Postcard
August 17, 1945

Dear folks— I'm on my way to Roswell New Mexico. Sorry I
didn't get to phone but didn't have time. Left about 11:00 a.m.
they pulled me off K.P. and gave me just a few minutes to get
ready. Love Bob

.————.

Postcard of Union Station in Kansas City, Missouri
August 19, 1945

Dear folks—we ate our breakfast here about 9:00 a.m. Today I'm
writing on the train—the Atchison Topeka and the Santa Fe is to
be exact. Love Bob

.————.

Western Union Telegram
August 18, 1945

DEAR FOLKS AM IN OMAHA NEBRASKA GOING TO ROSWELL NEW
MEXICO WEATHER TERRIBLY WARM LOVE = BOB.

.————.

CHAPTER 14

ROSWELL, NEW MEXICO

Squadron C-6 Box 1116
Roswell Army Air Field
Roswell, New Mexico
August 21, 1945

Dear folks:

What a day this has been. It has rained so hard this evening that water, ankle deep, is going down the streets like a mountain stream. Quite unusual from what I hear around these parts.

It sure was good to talk with you last night, Mom dear. Glad you, Pop, Kath and Neil are so well, etc. Keep it up.

Weather here has been very, very hot!! Boy oh boy! They weren't kidding when they said we could "sweat out" our discharges down here. This is a good base so far as barracks, P.X.s, etc. are concerned. Haven't gone to town as yet but don't think I'm missing much. I go to work at 7:00 a.m. tomorrow. I'll work on a section of the "line" called base flight. The "line" here and planes. We have B-29s, B-17s, A.T.6s, A.T.11s, C-47s, C-46Ss, basic trainers, etc.

I will work mostly on all except the B-29s. O.K. with me. I believe I'm going to like it here O.K. That is so far as work is concerned. Will work on many different kinds of planes for a change. Also work with a few W.A.C.s. Sort of fun after working with a bunch of guys all the time. There are several W.A.C.s and of course several jokers like me working on the "line." My barracks is very nice, a two-story job. Chow is pretty good, too. Just a poor state for the base, but won't help to worry about that.

I feel good and am having fun. I sent Kath and Neil a telegram for their wedding anniversary last night after talking with you. Glad you mentioned it, Mom dear. Thanks a million!!

I better sign off and get some sleep now.

Lots of love,

Bob (THE MEXICO KID)

.———.

August 29, 1945

Dear Mom and Dad:

I'm glad you folks have met the Joneses and the Gauswitzes. I know that Tom and Phil are just as glad as I am. We all knew that our folks would like each other a lot. The Jackson, Jones, Gauswitz and Gay combination just can't be beat!!!!

Wish I could have been at Uncle Dave's cottage with you last Sunday. Glad it was so much fun. Sounds as if they had really fixed the place up quite a bit.

Thanks for news about Alan, Bob K, and Bob Sasman. Sorry Pop, that you are having elevator trouble again.

Some general is here. The whole field stands retreat tonight. We fall out at 3:30 for roll call, march about one mile to big field in front of headquarters. The field about the size of one square block will be covered with officers, W.A.C.s, and enlisted men. What a mess!! The "meat wagons" keep plenty busy at retreat picking up the guys and girls who faint. The guys from the 8th Air Force are holding their own O.K.! Guess we like the sun.

All for now, lots of love,

Bob

.———.

September 2, 1945

Dear Mom and Pop:

Spent yesterday afternoon in town to keep from going nuts doing nothing. Ate a fairly good meal then went to a movie. It was called China Sky, a story of Pearl Buck I believe. Tonight, I saw the movie *Our Vines Have Tender Grapes* with Margaret O'Brien, Edward G. Robinson, etc. It was an excellent show and was about the lives of Norwegian farmers in Wisconsin. Madison, Kenosha, and Aurora were mentioned casually here and there.

Tomorrow we have another day off so guess I'll just sit around again. Might go into town and see another movie for something to do.

Roswell is New Mexico's third-largest city and we all agree that it is pretty sad! Quite a few Mexicans in town. The town is maybe 25 or 30,000 in population. The business district is mainly on one street several blocks long.

This field is quite large and is permanent. Our barracks are two-story white wooden ones like the ones you saw when we went to Camp McCoy several weeks ago. They are really nice compared to Nissen huts or tar paper barracks like Truax has. I'll try to get a few snapshots around here one of these days. The camp has regular asphalt streets with parking space by the sides or in front of each barracks.

All in all, if you could forget the miles of empty flat desert all around, the base looks like a regular city with plenty of traffic; stop signs; 2 theaters; post exchange with ice cream, pop, clothes, jewelry, toilet articles, stationery, etc.; service club; library, etc. Actually the base seems more complete than the town, and still outside of going to a movie every other day there is little to do except read.

Although the sun is plenty hot I must admit that it is a good change from the damp cold of last winter in England.

Thanks for news about Dr. Gay, and the new buses. Hope to be home soon to go for a ride in one of them with you before many months go by. Watch for me in the funny paper when they decide to let the young kids out of this man's Army.

Mom, glad to hear that you and Pop play the old "Atchison Topeka and Santa Fe."

I work on a different shift than the W.A.C.s do so really don't know how good they are on the "line." By the way, I requested the 3:00 to 11 shift because we can sleep longer in the morning, never stay until 11:00, and I get to work on the B-17s, would rather work on them than the B-29s.

Thanks for all the interesting news. Time to hit the sack; good night, lots of love,

Bob

.————.

September 4, 1945

Dear Mom and Dad:

Another bright and sunny day here in the "land of enchantment," anyway that is what it says on the New Mexico car plates.

Received two good letters from you this morning, Mom. Thanks a lot! They are really full of good news. Glad you got another good letter from Jack Campbell's mother. So old Jamie is at Pratt, Kansas, eh!! Not such a bad spot, I guess. Still wish we were together. He's one darn good boy. "A hell of a fella!" as we used to say. I'm anxious to hear from him again. We sure had a lot of good laughs together. Someday I want to go to California to see him. I'll never forget "ol' Jamie."

It's good to hear that you folks took Grandma Gay for a nice ride the other day, and also that you went out to see Grandpa and Grandma Lee. Sorry Grandpa hurt his foot but glad all is O.K.

According to the latest dope we can get concerning discharge, the points have been lowered to 80 and are to go still lower fairly soon. Also, we will add our points up to August 31. That will give me 76 points. I hope very, very much to be home by Xmas. Gee, I can hardly imagine how it will feel to be a civilian again.

If you are getting a spell of hot weather again plus the humidity. That is worse than this dry heat. I couldn't help but smile when I read the part of your letter that says, "Mr. Gauswitz thinks I would make a good lawyer." I can hardly picture myself as a lawyer. A fellow has to be plenty smart to go through law

Bob kept track of who he wrote back to by marking the envelopes "answered."

school, and a lot smarter than ever to make a good lawyer, when he gets out of that school.

A guy can get plenty stupid in this Army and I hope I can get out before I lose my last marble. I've never thought about being a lawyer. Guess it's a good profession all right. Don't hardly think I'm the right sort of person to make a lawyer of—do you when you really think it over??

Time for our exercise, so all for now.

Love, Bob

———————.

September 5, 1945

Dear Mom and Dad:

One thing we can always count on down here is a nice "warm" sunny day.

Well, they have dropped the points to 80 and are counting up to September 2nd. That will give me 76 points, I believe. Now if they will only drop to the points to 75 I'll be eligible for discharge. I figure it will take several months yet, because they are so slow on this base. There are still guys here with 90 to 115 points. They should already be civilians. They just can't get me out fast enough to suit me!! Maybe I'm getting bitter or something but in my mind this is the most stupidly (or should I say inefficiently) run field I've ever been on. Here is a boy they couldn't get to make a career out of the Army for anything!!

There are more bitter guys here than you could imagine. All these fellows with over 85 points were supposed to be at separation centers before August 31. They are still here.

What burns everyone up is that a lot of the 2nd lieuts are getting out with only 28 or 30 points, they say they don't need them. They don't, eh! Well why in the ####!! don't they discharge them and draft them in as enlisted men, and make them sweat out the system like enlisted men do. No one can understand why these "wonder men" with a year to a year and a half (all in the States) should get to go home so easy and so soon. Oh well, what the heck—!

We take 3 hours of exercise per week. 1 hour a day on any 3 days we want them between Monday and Saturday. I've got two in for this week—just one more hour tomorrow and I will be done for this week.

Hope this letter doesn't sound too uncheerful. I really feel good and still have high hopes of being home this year.

Lots of love,

Bob

.———.

September 10, 1945

Dear Mom and Dad:

I really had a swell time yesterday on my trip to Carlsbad. We left here at 8:00 a.m., and two G.I. trucks and arrived at the Caverns about 11:00 a.m. It is around 100 mi. from here. The board seats were beginning to get rather hard by the time we got there. Well, anyway we went into the caverns about 11:30 a.m. (we and about 450 others) and walked for 2 and $\frac{1}{2}$ hours before arriving at the lunchroom 750 ft. below the surface. So we had some very welcome chow. (Two sandwiches, cake, orange, pop, potato chips, and even a napkin!) We left the lunch room at 2:30 to see more caverns farther along. About 3:30 we again reached the lunch room and elevators.

Elevators are going out only, as it is quite a climb going out. About 45 people besides me decided to walk out rather than sweat out the long line at the elevators. Surprising is it seems, most of the people who walked out were women. Now this isn't the main reason that I walked out, just felt like walking rather than standing in line for a ride. We got out about 4:15 p.m. The trip is from 6 to 8 miles long, goes down to 829 feet below the surface. Temperature is 56°.

We left the place at 5:00 p.m., stayed in Carlsbad for chow at any cafe we wanted. Arrived in camp at 9:00 p.m. Really had fun and passed a day in a hurry, saw something to remember and do feel fine. The caverns had 1,800 visitors yesterday. Pretty fair turnout, don't you think?

Got a nice letter from Kath today.

Love, Bob

—————

September 15, 1945

Dear Mother and Dad:

Just finished 24 hours of guard duty. Chased Hans, Fritz and a few of their German buddies while they worked. Tomorrow I guess I'll catch up on a little sleep and take in a movie.

I'm awfully glad Phil likes the wedding present so well, Mom. That makes everything just perfect. Thanks again for being such a wonderful Mom!! Best Mom in all the world!!!!!!

How is everything going for you, Pop? O.K. I hope!! Should be able to get help pretty easy before long from the sound of things. Lots of people are losing their fat war jobs so expect you will see some of your old employees coming in some of these days. Time will tell. Weather here is pretty nice now. Not too hot during the day and cool enough at night for two blankets.

All for now.

Lots of love,

Bob

—————

September 18, 1945

Dear folks:

Received your letter and front page of the *State Journal* today. Thanks for both.

If they really get on the ball with these new Air Force separation centers it shouldn't be so long now before we can get out. Although I still consider myself very, very lucky to get out by Xmas. It sure would be fun to be discharged from Truax! Where and when? We will have to wait and see.

Sounds as if fall weather is really in to stay there. There will still be many beautiful days before winter sets in. The trees should be turning color pretty soon and people will be burning leaves, etc. I love the year in all four seasons in Madison!

That bus strike must be a lulu! Lots of people going to lose a few inches around the waist walking for a change. Gee, if the cabs go on strike before the buses are running again. Wow!! More fun!!

When I get out of this Army I'm going to get Uncle John to help me pick out some colorful socks, and ties, too. Pop, you and I will get the shirts because they will have to shoot both of us unless we don't wear the same size anymore. After all the times I used to borrow one of your shirts then mine didn't fit the occasion or something. It's only fair to give you the same chance with my shirts. Between us we will have enough stuff so that we just can't go wrong.

We are pretty busy again as they just brought in about 65 more 80-6's, like the two-seater planes the junior Birdmen at Truax fly. Most of the radio trouble lately is between the headsets, know what I mean? Otherwise there isn't much of anything doing.

I'm in charge of the three to 11:00 shift temporarily as the regular guy is on furlough. I have two enlisted men and one W.A.C. working for me. Both men and W.A.C. are sgts. That's the way it goes.

I feel fine and all is O.K. around here. Hope everything and everyone at home are the same. Guess that about does it for today.

Lots of love,
Bob

•———————•

Note from Mom

We didn't hear again from Bob until he knocked on the front door.
  Our boy was home for good.

RESOURCES FOR VETERANS

CAMP HOMETOWN HEROES
A weeklong free camp experience for children of fallen U.S. servicemembers seven to seventeen years old.
https://www.camphometownheroes.org/

CAPTAIN JOHN D. MASON VETERAN PEER OUTREACH PROGRAM
Reducing veteran suicides by connecting veterans in need with mental health providers in the VA.
https://www.veteranpeeroutreach.org/

CENTER FOR VETERANS ISSUES
Provides housing and supportive services for veterans and their families.
https://www.cvivet.org/about-cvi/

COUNTY VETERAN SERVICE OFFICERS ASSOCIATION OF WISCONSIN (CVSOA)
Assists veterans in navigating issues as their advocate.
https://wicvso.org/

NATIONAL AMERICAN INDIAN VETERANS ASSOCIATION
Helps all Native warriors in obtaining due benefits and services for members
of all 574 federally recognized tribes.
NAIV National Vice Commander Joey Strickland, Ret. Col. Choctaw:
+1 225 588 1634
https://www.facebook.com/p/NAIV-National-American-Indian-
Veterans-100064370636594/

NATIVE AMERICAN VETERANS ASSOCIATION
Aids in veterans' transition from a warrior's journey to civilian.
https://www.navavets.org/

OBJECTIVE: VETERANS' SMILE
Raises funds to help veterans who do not have dental care through the VA.
https://www.objectiveveterans-smile.org/

USA CARES
Aims to reduce veteran suicides by providing monetary and skill-building
education to vets.
https://usacares.org/

VETSNET: WISCONSIN VETERANS NETWORK
Assists veterans and their families with housing, employment and other
immediate needs.
https://www.wisvetsnet.org/

ABOUT THE AUTHOR

Dannelle Gay is a Wisconsin native who has been writing about travel for over a decade under the moniker The Traveling Cheesehead. As an award-winning travel writer, regional TV host and published author, she loves telling the stories of unique people and places.

Visit us at
www.historypress.com